# Passive Income

*35 Best, Proven Business Ideas for Building Financial Freedom in the New Economy*

## PUBLISHED BY: Chandler Wright

## © Copyright 2019 - All rights reserved.

The content contained within this book may not be reproduced, duplicated or transmitted without direct written permission from the author or the publisher.

Under no circumstances will any blame or legal responsibility be held against the publisher, or author, for any damages, reparation, or monetary loss due to the information contained within this book. Either directly or indirectly.

Legal Notice:

This book is copyright protected. This book is only for personal use. You cannot amend, distribute, sell, use, quote or paraphrase any part, or the content within this book, without the consent of the author or publisher.

Disclaimer Notice:

Please note the information contained within this document is for educational and entertainment purposes only. All effort has been executed to present accurate, up to date, and reliable, complete information. No warranties of any kind are declared or implied. Readers acknowledge that the author is not engaging in the rendering of legal, financial, medical or professional advice. The content within this book has been derived from various sources. Please consult a licensed professional before attempting any techniques outlined in this book.

By reading this document, the reader agrees that under no circumstances is the author responsible for any losses, direct or indirect, which are incurred as a result of the use of information contained within this document, including, but not limited to, — errors, omissions, or inaccuracies

*Chandler Wright*

# Table of Contents

Your Free Gift ............................................................................... 5

Chapter 1 - What is Passive Income? ........................................ 6

Chapter 2 - How to Create Passive Income Streams ............. 9

Chapter 3- Passive Income Ideas ............................................ 15

    Idea #1 - Affiliate Marketing ............................................ 15

    Idea #2 - Blogging ............................................................. 19

    Idea #3 - Dropshipping .................................................... 22

    Idea #4 - Amazon FBA ..................................................... 26

    Idea #5 - Self Publishing ................................................. 29

    Idea #6 - Shopify .............................................................. 33

    Idea #7 - Freelance Virtual Assistant ............................ 36

    Idea #8 - Creating Online Courses ................................ 40

    Idea #9 - Building an Application ................................. 43

    Idea #10 - Online Auctions ............................................. 47

    Idea #11 - Online Survey ................................................. 50

    Idea #12 - Online Consultancy ....................................... 53

    Idea #13 – Cryptocurrency ............................................. 56

    Idea #14 - Make YouTube Videos ................................. 59

    Idea #15 - Online Fitness Instructor ............................. 64

    Idea #16 - Renting out space via AirBnB ..................... 68

    Idea #17 - Becoming a Silent Partner .......................... 71

Idea #18- Cashback Rewards with Credit Cards ... 74

Idea #19 - Renting Out Your Parking Spot ............ 77

Idea #20 - Network Marketing .............................. 80

Idea #21 - Storage Rentals ...................................... 83

Idea #22 - Develop Design Elements ..................... 86

Idea #23 - Website Domain Flipping ..................... 89

Idea #24 - Selling T-Shirts Online ......................... 92

Idea #25 - Placing Ads on Your Car ....................... 95

Idea #26- Using Instagram for Passive Income .... 98

Idea #27- Facebook Marketing ............................. 103

Idea #28- Create a Podcast ................................... 107

Idea #29 - Buy an Existing Online Business ........ 109

Idea #30- Franchise a Business ............................. 113

Idea #31- Rent out your clothes ............................ 116

Idea #32- Develop WordPress Themes ................. 118

Idea #33- Launch a Webinar ................................. 121

Idea #34- Give Fashion & Product Reviews ........ 124

Idea #35- Help Someone Learn a Language through Skype .................................................................. 126

Conclusion ....................................................................... 129

Thank you ........................................................................ 130

*Chandler Wright*

# Your Free Gift

As a way of saying thanks for your purchase, I wanted to offer you two free bonuses - *"The Fastest Way to Make Money with Affiliate Marketing"* and *"Top 10 Affiliate Offers to Promote"* cheat sheets, exclusive to the readers of this book.

To get instant access just go to:

https://theartofmastery.com/chandler-free-gift

Inside the cheat sheets, you will discover:
- The fastest way to start generating income with affiliate marketing
- My top 10 favorite affiliate offers to promote for high recurring commissions
- Access to a FREE live training where you will learn:
- how one affiliate marketer built a $500,000 a month business all while traveling the world...
- The 3-step system to eliminate risk and instability in your online business
- The 7 biggest mistakes affiliates make in making money online
- How tech companies are giving away FREE MONEY to help you start
- And much more...

# Chapter 1 - What is Passive Income?

Earn money while you sleep? That strategy sounds like a dream, doesn't it?

The idea of passive income has been a goal for many, and it has long been the ideal way of generating income for entrepreneurs looking to generate a healthy income, without working the traditional 40-hour weeks and dealing with the pressures of daily duties and accompanying responsibilities

When an income revenue is passive, it means that you do the work upfront once, and it requires very little or no maintenance to keep the money flowing. This doesn't mean that maintenance can be forgotten or completely ignored. Most passive income models still require some sort of maintenance, and it is critical as an entrepreneur to track every bit of passive income you have, no matter how automated it is.

Passive income is real, and it certainly is achievable. In my early 20s, I was able to build a business that currently generates over six figures a year passively. But for those who never built a business before, the fear of uncertainty and failure can cause them to not take action.

Once achieved, passive income is great, but to getting there certainly isn't easy. You definitely need to invest some amount of time to get things started: and the truth is, time is far more valuable than money because time can only be spent once, then it is gone forever, unlike money which can be earned over every time.

Before we transition and cover the many aspects of passive income ideas that you can create to automate your revenue, we must first understand the concept of passive income and what it is and is not. You'll find plenty of posts on the web talking about ideas of passive income, how to go about it, and what it takes to get there but they never really go in depth. In this book, we're covering each one in extensive details.

- Passive Income and Interest

When money is lent in an S-corporation or into a partnership acting as a pass-through entity by the owner of that entity, the interest gained on that loan into the portfolio income qualifies as passive income. According to the IRS, self-charged interest can be treated as passive income or passive activity deductions, only if the loan proceeds are utilized in a passive activity.

- Passive Income and Property

Very often, rental properties are considered passive income. There are a few exceptions to this rule, though. If you're a real estate professional dealing solely in properties, then the income you make on the rental is actually your active income. Also, rental income is not considered passive income if you're self-renting. It does not constitute passive income unless the lease has been signed before 1988.

- Passive Income and the No Material Inclusion

If an investor invests $100,000 in a bicycle store with the agreement that the investor gets a percentage of the earnings by the owners, this venture would be passive income for the investor, as long as the investor doesn't contribute or participate actively in the business operation, other than placing an investment.

The true benefit of passive income lies in the records of profits or loss. When a taxpayer records a loss as a passive activity, only the passive activity profits can be deducted instead of the entire income as a whole. It's wise for a person to ensure that all his or her passive activities are classified as passive activities, so that one can make the most out of tax deductions.

- Passive Income and Grouping Activities

Grouping activities happen when a person groups two or more of one's passive activities into a larger one. This forms the 'appropriate economic unit.' According to the IRS, when a taxpayer does this, they would only have to provide material participation for the activity as a whole and not in multiple activities.

# Chapter 2 - How to Create Passive Income Streams

It's not hard to understand what passive income means. While it's easy to understand the concept, it does require work to produce the results. Passive income requires some form of investment of time, energy, and of course, money to make it worth the long run of minimal maintenance ahead.

Based on the Internet's capabilities, building a passive income stream has made this process easier. There are plenty of online passive income ideas you can embark in, and I personally believe the internet is the best place to start. So how do you create successful passive income revenues? In this chapter, we'll explore how to go about creating a plan to produce this form of income, especially now that we have a better idea of what passive income is.

It may not be easy, but it's worth the effort. Here are some step-by-step ways to ensure you're on the right path to acquire and work on your own passive income stream:

## Step 1 - It starts with an idea

Of course, the first thing you should do is select the idea which you can work on the best. Later in the book we'll discuss 35 business models that you can generate passive income with. I recommend you pick one from there. Which one you decide on is entirely an individual decision as it involves the unique situation including your passion, interest, skill sets, etc. If you have the means to purchase real estate or business investing or even in dividend stocks, then great. If not, you can look at other choices you have. For most people now, passive income is built from an online business. One of the biggest reasons being that there are plenty of ways that you can create passive income online that doesn't require such a huge investment upfront. So, go through the business models listed in this book, then start by writing down which one works best with your situation now, and identify what resources you have to make this idea happen.

## Step 2: Setting your goals

When you've selected on the passive income business you want to build, your next step is to set measurable goals and to start taking action. You need to invest a good deal of time to bring your idea to fruition, so you'll want to do proper research to make sure you understand as much as you can about the business.

I recommend everyone to purchase a proven course/program on the chosen business model and start following it. There are courses on almost everything right now. All you need is the willingness to research and to start implementing what you learn.

It's also vital to clearly write down your goals because setting goals on pen and paper are much more powerful than setting them in your mind. Setting goals arbitrarily in your mind will often lead to failure. Keep in mind though, failing is ok and a normal part of the process. It serves as a learning experience for you to get better and push you towards success. So set your goals, take action, and keep failing forward towards your goal.

## Step 3- Planning your Steps to get there

Once you've decided on your passive income business as well as set some hard goals, it's now time to plan effective steps on reaching these goals. How will you achieve goal one? How will you get from point A to point B? What can you do to get there? What are the actions you need to take?

Again, you've articulated all these steps onto paper, so it'll help you bring the gap between dream and reality a little closer. Keep in mind that nothing materializes quickly - if it does, then it'll burn out just as quickly. Don't chase get rich quick schemes, as the business also disappears quickly. Make sure you're selecting a business that is proven to last for the long-term, like the ones I list in this book. The step by step plan you put into place must be consistent and persistent and as long as you know what's going to take you to get there, you're setting yourself up for success!

## Step 4 - Have Income Backup Plans

Creating and beginning your journey towards financial freedom can be daunting, and it can be easy to give up after not seeing the results you want initially and instead focus on work that gives you consistent pay (like a job). It might take a while to build, but once you've successfully established your passive income stream, the rewards are great. You'll achieve not only more money, but more time and location freedom as well. On the journey to get there, however, you need backup plans. Getting into your passive income stream without any monetary backup plan is a fool's game.

In the entrepreneurship space currently, especially online, you'll commonly hear many so called "guru's" preaching to people that you need to go ALL IN. That you need to quit your job, invest all your life savings, wake up at 5am, go to bed at 2am, and work on your business 16 hours a day.

Many people who've never built a business before overestimate how much it takes to actually do so, thus, believing in BS advice like this. Yes, you have to put in a lot of time, effort, and sometimes money (depending on the business you've chose), but doing it like this going "all in" will only lead to a burn out. What's more important than a short burst of massive work is CONSISTENCY. It's much better to put in a consistent, focused few hours a day while maintaining your normal life, rather than dropping everything for your business. This is actually most successful people built their businesses, so don't get tricked by the lies the few "guru's" that are vocal that you see online.

Ok enough of my rant, let's get back into the topic. Like I said, you need to keep your active income and just work on your passive income on the side, slowly and steadily building it up till it reaches a point that enables you to quit your active income if you want to, and rely on your passive one. However, completely retiring at that point is still not a wise decision. It's smart to continue reinvesting your profits and creating other passive incomes sources, so that you don't rely on just one source of income.

*Passive Income Ideas*

Be sure to always have a fallback plan, even if your passive income pays your bills and feeds you more than what your active income can bring to the table. You always want to be ready for the change in the market, and seeking new opportunities. If you do keep your active income work but work on passive income on the side, you can slowly and steadily build it up. For example, if you're starting a new blog, don't quit your day job. You can make a ton of money from blogging, but not many people do, and it takes time to get there. In sum, be sure you have a fallback plan until that passive income source is paying your bills.

## Step 5 - Exemplify Successful Online Marketers

Online marketers are good examples of people who build passive income streams. In fact, many successful online marketers usually have multiple different passive income revenues. If you're trying to succeed in business, you'll want to be like an investigator. Seek out those who are successful and learn exactly what they are doing. Then all you need to do is to do the same thing, to get the same results. You don't have to reinvent the wheel here. Ask yourself, what and how are the most successful online marketers doing to generate passive income? How have they managed to build their sales funnels and sell products on autopilot? Do plenty of research prior to starting your own online passive income stream. Some people teach you to just get started and figure it out later. I don't believe in this approach. I always like to take the time to research and really get a good idea of the business before I dive in and get started. The time you invest to gain the knowledge, understanding, and wisdom will be worth it.

## Step 6 - Join mastermind Groups

Apart from learning from the master online marketers, another step I encourage is to join online (or offline) communities with other entrepreneurs and form a mastermind. You can search on places such as on LinkedIn, Reddit, Facebook, as well as networking groups offline, which you can find by using google, meetup.com or attending business seminars.

When I was making around $1000 a month from my online business, I decided to invite 3 other people I knew who were in the same business making around the same income and formed a little mastermind facebook chat group. We talked everyday and shared everything from new strategies we tried, what worked, what didn't, etc. All four of us were making around $1000 a month when we started, but in about a year, we were all making over $10,000 a month. I believe being in a mastermind was one of the single biggest factor of succeeding in my business. I formed mine with others who were making around the same income, but if you can collaborate with a mastermind with those who are more successful than you, that is better.

As the famous quote by Jim Rohn asserts, "You are the average of the 5 people you spend the most time with." This premise recommends the more time you spend with those who have already built passive income streams, the faster it'll accelerate your results as well.

Ask as many questions as you can (without being annoying) and more often than not, someone in the group would be happy to share knowledge and expertise. People often perceive successful people as "greedy," but in reality you'll find that they're normal people just like you and me and are happy to help you whenever they can. You'll also notice that you don't have to be a genius to become successful, and will help you feel confident that you can also build a successful business as well. You might even end up buying an online business or even partnering up in a business with someone in your mastermind - Remember, your network is your net worth. Gather tips, tactics, strategies, and advice to help you along your journey.

## Step 7 - Find a mentor

On your path to success, you may hit stumbling blocks and get frustrated. It happens. Being in groups and learning second-hand from successful people who've built passive income streams is one thing but having a mentor guide you every step of the way is by far the fastest way to creating the same results yourself. Being in your groups and forums helps as you can find a suitable mentor along the way. But keep in mind that many people, especially online marketers, portray success, when in reality only a few actually achieve it. What's worse is that these same people will sell mentorship/coaching packages for a ton of money. You don't want to pay these people for mentorship obviously, as they haven't even achieved success themselves.

When you do find someone whom you can connect with and has a few successful businesses under his or her belt, ask if you can take mentorship with this figure. This person may take you up on your offer. Do not get discouraged if you don't find one - good things come to those who wait. It's better to take your time in forming a good partnership with a reliable mentor than to hastily connect with one who's not a good mentor at all.

## Step 8 - Scale like the wind

The last but certainly not least, of things to do in creating your passive income stream is to scale. When you find a business that works and you start making money, you need to start scaling like the wind. Part of ensuring that your revenue stream is sustainable is making it scalable. The good thing about passive income is that it can be scaled whether it's a blog, online courses, or audiobooks. All you need to do is reinvest back into what's working and scale. It won't happen right away but through persistence, you'll reach the goals you want.

# Chapter 3- Passive Income Ideas

## Idea #1 - Affiliate Marketing

**What Is Affiliate Marketing?**

Affiliate marketing is the process of earning a sum of commission by promoting someone else's products or company. If you find a product you like, you promote it to your channels, and in the process, earn a piece of profit for every sale that you make. You make a commission each time you share, recommend, or promote another person's product, service, or company. Each time that company gets a sale, you get a cut! The great part about affiliate marketing is that you do not need to create your own product or company or invest the time and effort into something to sell it.

**Who is it for?**

Affiliate marketing is perfect for those who need to work from home. It's an ideal home business simply because it doesn't require much costs to get started and you do not need to stock or ship or produce any kind of product, inventory, or even do any delivery or service. You get paid for referring new clients and customers. While affiliate marketing isn't hard, it still requires some knowledge, a bit of planning, and consistent effort to make it worthwhile and yield significant income.

**How much money can you potentially earn?**

An affiliate marketer's payment depends largely on the commissions they receive from the company that they acquaint themselves with. Buttons, links, and banners of the product that they sell contain unique user ID embedded into the HTML code of your blog to enable ads to that business appear. Essentially, an affiliate marketer can earn anywhere from $300 a day to even up to $3,000 a day or more; this profit depends entirely on how much effort they put in and what their profit goals are.

**How does affiliate marketing works?**

- **Find Your Niche -** Your niche should be a product or service that you have knowledge on or something that you**'re** passionate about because then you'd already have an idea on whom to target, how it works, what methods to use, and so on. This niche does not need a mass audience as long as there's some kind of audience looking for the product or service, you're good to go.

- **Research & Identify Affiliate Opportunities-** Once you've selected your niche, it's now time to look for affiliate partners. These are the companies that will pay you to promote their businesses on your site. Most affiliate programs are free to join and you can find them in many ways such as through affiliate marketplaces like Rakuten and ShareASale. You can also join affiliate programs such as Amazon Associates and Overstock and sponsored post programs like Blogvertise.

- **Build Your Website -** A website is an integral part of affiliate marketing especially if you want most of your work and marketing to be done online. Your website is a key component that acts as your marketing channel as well as the home base for your business. There are plenty of website services available currently that allow you to create a website easily such as WIX or SquareSpace.

- **Create Affiliate Content -** Once you have your website, it's time to assess the content you will feature. Start crafting authentic content that speaks about your niche and promotes your affiliate products. You can work on various types of content ranging from product reviews to How-To Guides, recipes, and even do give-away discounts.

- **Add Marketing Channels to Extend Your Reach** - Your website shouldn't be your online means of marketing online. Affiliate marketing needs to be split across different marketing channels as this is an ideal way to target, reach, and build your audience. Once you start your website, connect it to your social media channels and blog. Once you've gained a substantial amount of following, start a newsletter, too. People prefer reading about certain information on specific platforms.

## Myths about Affiliate Marketing

- **It's Easy** - So what are the myths about affiliate marketing? You've probably heard about them during your research. Firstly, by the way it's described, it sounds like affiliate marketing is easy. The truth is, it becomes easier once you learn the process. But managing affiliate marketing is probably the easiest aspect. Other than that, affiliate marketing is competitive and time-consuming. There are no shortcuts to this and you need to put a good amount of hard work to get the ball rolling.

- **Plenty of traffic means plenty of profit** - Many newbies think that their main marketing goal is to continuously drive traffic to their website. While this is important, it isn't the only thing you can and should world on. It is also about how appealing your target market feels about your product which would then increase your sales ratio. Advertising at the right channels where your target audience is one way to get their buy-in.

- **Popularity on Social media ensures success -** You may be popular on social media to attract a new audience and reach a wider depth. But customers want to buy your product and will continue buying your product simply because they deem it as good quality and also meets their desired specification.

# Idea #2 - Blogging

## What is blogging?

The term "blogging" has evolved since its inception. In fact, it's more than just a personal online diary and its uses have evolved dramatically from an avenue where you just write your stuff down on a daily basis to a medium of income, news, and information. Even the appearance of blogs has changed from merely an online diary to now a site that has exciting marketing and social features. ProBlogger describes a blog as a type of website that displays content in chronological order. While the very essence of blogging still remains to this day, you need a variety of skills in 2019 to run a successful and sustainable blog, from not only knowing to write engagingly but also the aptitude to use visuals and PNG files and buttons and links as well as the ability to market your blog professionally.

## Who is it for?

Blogs are for anyone and everyone who wants to talk about a certain topic or document something, curate information, and generally craft and share their views, opinions, daily life, and just about any topic under the sun. Anyone can open a blog, but it also takes a great deal to keep it sustainable with new and fresh content. Blogs are great for startup companies, tech companies, bakery stores, hobbyists, photographers, crafters, event planners, marketers, doctors, ballerinas - anyone. As long as you have content to write and talk about, then blogs are a perfect platform to do that.

## How much money can you potentially earn?

When blogging was relatively new, carving out your name on internet retail space was relatively easy. Now, it takes a little bit more work because the market is saturated with blogs of various kinds. Many of today's blog income earners have been building their blogs back when it was still new. It's a different story altogether, but the cash flow is lucrative still, albeit a little harder to get. It's not something that you can get rich quickly, even if you do work on your blog full-time. If you want to make a living out of blogging, you need to do some really good research and work on content that appeals and sells. According to a survey done by Blogger.com in 2012 found that 17% of bloggers could sustain their lifestyle and family through their blogs, whereas, 81% never even made $100. The balance of 2% spent less than 2 hours blogging but made $150k. ProBlogger also conducted a survey among bloggers and found that 9% made $1000 to $10,000 a month but the vast majority made less than $3.50 per day. How much you make depends on several factors, such as how often you blog, how competitive the topic is, and your effectiveness of building an audience and also generate the right traffic. Success will not come quickly.

## How does blogging work?

**Step 1 -** Open an account in any blogging site you like:

1. WordPress.org
2. Wix
3. WordPress.com
4. Blogger
5. Tumblr
6. Medium
7. Squarespace
8. Ghost

**Step 2 -** Choose the kind of layout you want.

**Step 3 -** Customize your blog according to your needs, content you plan on posting, and interest

**Step 4 -** Click on New Post and start writing your content. It's that easy!

## Myths about Blogging

- Blogging is just a quick fad - By now you already know that it's not a fad. The landscape of blogging has changed quite a bit and even Fortune 500 companies use blogs. Blogs can drive actual and profitable business so long as you're willing to work on them.

- Your posts should never be over 500 words - It's false. Your blog post can be over 500 words as long as it's engaging and something your readers want to know. Having in-depth articles on your blog actually improves your SEO rankings so don't worry about your word count but instead worry about the quality of the content.

- If you can't write well, you can't blog - You may have an English degree but that does not mean you are a great writer. There are different kinds of audience looking for various things only and different ways of indulging in content. Depending on who your target audience is, as well as the kind of content you want to write about, you don't necessarily need high-end college-worthy writing skills.

- You can't write a blog post in an hour - Every piece on your blog does not have to be a masterpiece and it doesn't need to be a certain amount of words. You write because you have things to say on your blog and as long as they serve the value your audience is looking for: you can take any amount of time to write engaging, purposeful content.

# Idea #3 - Dropshipping

## What is Dropshipping?

Dropshipping is an element of retail fulfillment practice in the standard retail model that allows a store selling products and merchandise to not hold its own inventory; in other words, do away with keeping their products in stock, or shipping their products to their customers on their own or owning a warehouse to store its products. In this case, whenever there's an order for the product, the seller purchases its item from a third-party vendor and this third-party vendor ships it directly to the customer. This retailer partner with a dropship supplier does the manufacturing, warehousing, packaging, and shipping of these products on the retailer's behalf. The merchant doesn't see or handle the said product.

## Who is Dropshipping For?

If you're a first timer entering the online business, then drop shipping is a great business model to begin with initially. It's low-risk and low-investment which is great for novices starting their business. It doesn't involve much monetary gamble. It's ideal for someone who is the current owner of a retail store and already has an inventory, but looking to reach newer, wider markets. This business model, however, doesn't give you amazing results from the get-go. Dropshipping margins are relatively lower so this might not bode well for a startup brand because these businesses do not have ultimate control where customer satisfaction related to brand experience and branding is concerned.

## How much money can you potentially earn?

Depending on how much work you put into and the effort of time and some money, you can earn anywhere from $1,000 to $1,000,000 in a year or more. For example, if you get a product at $15 and you sell it on your site for $30. Minus the shipping and advertising costs, your profit is $10. To make $100,000 in a year, you need to sell at least 1000 products each month. This means $10 x 1000 orders = $10,000 per month. You can potentially earn $120,000 if your idea, product, and strategies work well.

## How does Dropshipping work?

- **Finding your Niche in Dropshipping** - It may sound overwhelming to find your niche in business because there are plenty of things that you can get involved in at first. An evergreen niche is a niche that most retailers would like - it stands the test of time. Things like gaming, beauty, fashion, and weight loss are very evergreen niches. However, on the other hand, trending niches have instant profits and surge, but it also falls in popularity pretty fast.

- **Looking and Finding the Right suppliers** - In the world of dropshipping, it's critical to work with the right supplier, especially since suppliers are a crucial element of this entire drop shipping process. But like everything in life, drop shipping suppliers also come in different sizes, needs, and interests. To identify good suppliers is to place small orders to get a sense of their processes, sales reps, and professionalism. This way, you can pinpoint:
    - How efficient their ordering process is
    - How fast items are shipped out
    - How efficient they are in following up with an invoice for tracking information
    - How good the quality of their packing is

- **Setting up your Business** - One of the biggest pull factors is that you don't need stock or even to handle the things that you are selling and you can also start with limited funds. In its very basic idea, dropshipping requires a website optimized for e-commerce and ad from the merchant you purchase items from a third party supplier who then fulfills an order made by a customer on your e-commerce website. This cuts operational costs and also frees up your time to focus on other aspects of the business such as customer acquisition - marketing and promoting your website. A site optimized for e-commerce is extremely crucial in the drop shipping business model. One of the simplest platforms that you can use is Shopify, as it comes with built-in, customizable apps to help you create a website, increase sales, and even market your website. It's a very easy plug-and-play option.

## Myths about Dropshipping

- **Dropshipping only works for low priced, general products -** The truth is, dropshipping now offers entrepreneurs looking to sell something the ability to offer specialized, high-quality items. If you find a niche for your products, you've definitely found a market that values quality products.

- **You need to have an in-depth understanding of coding and all things IT-**Any knowledge can be beneficial for your business but you don't need to be a tech-expert to run a dropshipping site. The basic idea of crafting a well working site as well as knowledge in marketing can help you kick off your business. Over time, as you gain knowledge and expertise as well as money, you can hire experts to help you fine-tune your business.

- **All you need is to list products on your site and the sales will roll in -** If that were true, then anyone can make a living with dropshipping. Unless you've hit the golden ticket with your product, chances of getting a profit immediately are quite dim. Dropshipping is not a get-rich scheme. It takes time to build and reach markets as well as target audiences. However, once you've got your footing, it'll be much easier.

## Idea #4 - Amazon FBA

### What is Amazon FBA?

On Amazon's FBA site, you'll see the tagline - you sell it, we ship it. The Fulfillment by Amazon, or for short, FBA, is a process where you store your products in Amazon's fulfillment centers, and they'll pick your products, pack it for you, and ship it for you as well as provide customer service for these products. When you list your products on FBA, customers are eligible for free shipping and qualified listings are shown using the Prime logo. Customers browsing your site know that Amazon will do the packing, delivery, and everything for the product.

### Who is Amazon FBA for?

If you love shopping and also love taking advantage of amazing shopping deals, then you might want to look into starting a business that can bring your extra income. Amazon FBA gives the opportunity to earn money all through shopping for items and then reselling them. If you like certain products on Amazon and you'd like to sell them, you can do it via Amazon FBA but you don't need to worry about storage or customer support, sales, or shipping because Amazon does this step for you.

### How much money can you potentially earn?

It depends on the amount of inventory you begin with because your profits will vary. With a good strategy, you can earn a good few thousand dollars in your first month of selling on FBA and up to $10,000 or more a few months later as you scale your business.

## How does Amazon FBA work?

### Step 1- Set up FBA

You can start by setting up your 'Selling on Amazon' account and then add FBA account to this. You can set up your account at this link.
https://sellercentral.amazon.com/

### Step 2- Set up your product listings

Here, you can add the products you want to sell to the Amazon catalog either one at a time or in bulk. You can also integrate your inventory-management software using Amazon's API.

### Step 3- Preparing your products

All your listed products need to be 'e-commerce' ready, so that Amazon can safely and securely transport them to the customer's location. You can also get Amazon's preferred prep and shipping supplies if you ever need it delivered right to your location.

### Step 4- Shipping your products to Amazon

Here, you need to create your shipping plans and also look into discounted partner carriers. You can use your partners to ship and track your shipments to Amazon fulfillment centers where Amazon's online seller tools can help you through the process.

### Step 5- Ordering, picking, packing, and shipping

When customers order your products, Amazon picks it up, packs it, and ships it for you. Prime Amazon customers get fast and free shipping on your products. However, all customers can qualify for free shipping on orders that are eligible. Orders are quickly and efficiently filled using web-to-warehouse, high-speed picking and sorting system from Amazon. Customers will receive tracking information directly from Amazon.

## Step 6- Customer support all throughout the way

The great aspect about using Amazon FBA is that they offer amazing customer-service that provides inquiries, refunds, and returns on their orders on Amazon marketplace. This service is provided 24 hours a day, seven days every week.

# Idea #5 - Self Publishing

## What is self-publishing?

Self-publishing is publishing your own book using platforms such as Amazon Kindle. As a self-publishing author, you need to produce your final draft, supply the funds to design your book, market the book on your own, as well as distribute the book. You also get to decide how many copies should be printed and how much each would cost.

E-book publishing has opened up a new avenue for authors as online readership keeps growing the more and more people are moving away from regular books to online reading. Self-publishing eliminates the costs involved with printing and distributing physical copies, and it is also accessible worldwide.

## Who is it for?

Self-publishing is useful for authors who cannot get a publisher or agent. This option is also ideal for people who have marketing prowess, which means there are times that you need to give your book away for free or publish your book in series or even look into effective marketing strategies that traditional publishers may not be aware of.

The money you earn from self-publishing could also be much better. Most authors price their books slightly cheaper or even the first of the series is free and charge the others at a certain price. It's also great for people who love writing and would like their books published on an online avenue and have a niche audience read their books.

## How much money can you potentially earn?

Like all the other passive income methods listed here, self-publishing is also not an easy path to make a huge amount of money overnight. The Self-published author has the potential to make over $100,000 a year if the business is built correctly; and that's also because many self-published authors have plenty of books already published and collectively they make the amount.

Some authors also end up making less than $500 a year. With a publisher, you could end up with 10% or less but when you self-publish, you can keep 50 to 90% of the profits and this also depends on the distribution channel you use. If you use Amazon Kindle Direct Publishing (KDP), it gives you 30 to 70% to authors.

## How Self-Publishing Works

Self-publishing is like building a house entirely on your own, with little to no help. It is actually quite satisfying to write your own book and publish it and create an audience that loves your work. In today's market, there are several ways to publish your book.

Essentially, here are the basics of self-publishing your book:

**Step 1- Write your book -** Of course, you need to start with writing your book. Pick your genre, write your draft, and work on your book.

**Step 2- Edit your Manuscript -** Self-edit your manuscript as much as you can. Enlist the help of reliable friends and colleagues who have the gift of word and grammar to help you analyze your words, sentences, and even your story.

**Step 3- Designing the cover and formatting of the interior-** The cover of your self-published book helps sell it and authors of both kinds of publishing - the traditional versus the online ones all heavily depend on a well-designed book. You can hire the services of a designer of UpWork or Fiverr for a small fee or you can even use online design services such as Canva or Pressbooks.

**Step 4- Self Publish your Book in Print or as an Ebook-** Before the internet, if you want to self-publish a book, you'd have to get a print run done which would involve paying up front for thousands of copies of books to be printed. You run into a risk of having copies of books you struggle to sell. Thankfully, with the internet, you can simply publish your book on Amazon's Kindle Direct Publishing. You can also Print-On-Demand through either KDP or IngramSpark or offer your book as an eBook.

**Step 5- Master the Kindle Store -** Mastering the Kindle store is akin to understanding and mastering other online platforms that you use to advertise, talk, and market yourself or your blog. Just like every other online platform nowadays, Kindle also has its own set of algorithms and knowing this will help you understand what works and what doesn't when you publish your book.

You must also know what a good price range for your book would be, so it will sell, as well as how to compose a good book description. The latter is key as it's the first contact for a potential reader of your book.

**Step 6- Marketing your Book efficiently and effectively -** For people to know your book and to reach the audience that wants to read your content, you need to craft a creative and effective marketing strategy. Employ different routes of marketing from social media to digital media, email marketing to on-ground meet and greet. All of this will enable you to get to know your audience and learn from whatever tips and mistakes you might make.

**Myths about Self-Publishing**

- **You can tell if a book is self-published -** Unless the book has plenty of errors, a badly designed cover and margins that do not exist, it is hard to tell if the book is self-published or not. Just because you're a self-publisher doesn't mean you have to do everything on your own. Your expertise lies in writing, but you can always get help from family and friends to help you in fields where you expertise, such as designing and editing. You can also easily hire an editor or book designer, should your budget permit, to look through the final draft of your book before you click on Publish.

- **Publishers do not like Self-Published authors -** This is a huge myth, one that needs to be squashed. A self-published author who has hit success will make publishing houses notice you, and it will also tell them that there's a market for the genre of your book. It also tells everyone in publishing that you've got what it takes to not only write a book but market it as well. You might just end up with a full-fledged publishing deal.

- **Self-Publishing is just an author being vain –** Oh, how the mind runs. There's more to self-publishing than just satisfying one's sense of importance. Self-publishing gives life to books nobody thought had a readership. While publishers do have their area of expertise, they will, more often than not, stick to certain types of genres that guarantee a mass following. Publishers also have specific capacities regarding the number of books they can assume in a year, which means books with merit are excluded.

- **Self-Publishing is merely the process of making a book -** The real work really begins once you have a self-published book. For any author, the biggest challenge would be to sell, distribute, and market your book, and most of the time, book stores and distributors prefer to work with publishing companies and not authors. This also means that self-published authors need to look at other means to get their books to their intended target audience and it takes a great deal of hard work to get there. So, when you're writing your book, you should also look into how to sell and market your book.

# Idea #6 - Shopify

### What is Shopify?

Shopify is a platform that offers potential retailers a comprehensive e-commerce site where they can create, design, promote, and sell products to customers in any part of the globe. This platform comes with plenty of ready-to-go templates that will suit your business needs and the products or services you plan to sell. Due to its use and integration of today's popular applications and practices, Shopify is a fast growing crowd favorite. For example, it utilizes 70 payment gateways with checkouts in over 50 languages, making product sales quick and hassle-free for customers anywhere in the world.

### Who is it for?

Shopify is a form of drop shipping and it is great for novices starting their own business. It doesn't involve much monetary gamble. It's ideal for someone who is the current owner of a retail store and already has an inventory, but looking to reach newer, wider markets. Shopify is a plug-and-play e-commerce store. They have all the necessary tools, plug-ins, and templates that enable anyone to open and operate an e-commerce store.

### How much money can you potentially earn?

To put it briefly, if you're only selling one digital product, then Shopify may not be the platform for you. You would be better off using a PayPal button or even a WooCommerce plug-in on your blog. However, if you're planning to run a full-fledged online store that requires a multi-product e-commerce support with inventory, customer records, marketing tools, and so on, then Shopify is the go-to platform for you, which will definitely be worth your investment.

Depending on how much effort you put in, your Shopify store can bring you anywhere from around $500 to $100,000. There are plenty of successful Shopify stores which you can use as examples, however, keep in mind that you'll only reap what you sow, so your success rate depends on how much time and effort you're willing to put into your shop.

## How does Shopify Work?

### Step 1- Setting Up your Shopify Store

To start with Shopify, you must first sign up for an account. Visit Shopify.com. You'll see a signup form. Use the form to create an account. Enter all the details required and ensure that they're accurate. Afterward, click the **'Create your store now'** button. At this step, you must select a Unique Store Name, as well as your preferred store template, and include all necessary details.

### Step 2- Add Your Products to the Store

It's time to add your products to the store! To do this step, navigate to the bar on the left of the store and select **'Products'**. You'll then see **'Add a product'** in the top right corner of the page. You can use this screen to add in the details of your product. Put in relevant details for your product and focus on words and texts that can help with SEO such as description, name as well as URL. Include as much information as possible so your customers are informed of your products, but you don't need to write a long story. Succinct and useful information is the best.

### Step 3- Selecting your preferred payment gateway

With a payment gateway set in place, your customers can make their payments via your website. Different gateways have different prices and commission rates, so it's important to know what features each gateway offers before taking on their service. Not all payment gateways are equal as they all serve different needs and interests.

## Step 4- Get Your Online Shop "LIVE"

A few more details are required before your site can go live. These details are about your company and how you plan to make your product deliveries as well as pay your taxes. Once you're done entering all these details, test your site from purchasing an item to shipping an item and using your payment gateways. When you're satisfied with the results, click enable to make your site go LIVE!

## Myths about Shopify

- **Shopify is a rigid platform** - If you're are worried that Shopify doesn't give you room to explore and expand your e-commerce site, just take a quick look at all the successful online retailers and what they did with their own sites. Shopify does seem rigid to the advance CMS builder but for novices and people who want a built-in an e-commerce site with minimal coding and HTML headaches, Shopify can do this and so much more.

- **You cannot integrate Shopify with advance back-end systems** - As your shop grows, you'll want it to look more polished and offer more user-friendly features to make shopping, searching, and purchasing easier. Shopify knows this which is why you CAN integrate Shopify's platform with more sophisticated CRMs such as Salesforce or ERPs such as NetSuite.

# Idea #7 - Freelance Virtual Assistant

**What Is It?**

As the name indicates, a freelance virtual assistant is an individual who is hired by a business to assist with either the daily tasks of the business or a specific role from a remote location. Many small businesses, as well as online platforms, typically seek virtual assistants to help with these roles so that they may do away with the need to hire additional staff into their workforce. A function of a virtual assistant is vast and dependant on the nature of the business interested in hiring a virtual assistant. It can range from replying emails, clerical work, or managing personal schedules. At times, the job role for a virtual assistant is quite specific and can encompass the following responsibilities, depending on the hiring business:

1. Managing Social Media Accounts
2. Market Research
3. Finance Management
4. Content Creator
5. Web Design
6. Writer
7. Personal Assistant

**Who Is It For?**

Those who take up the option of becoming a virtual assistant are usually those individuals who fall into one of the following categories:

- You have the freedom to work from anywhere and are not confined to any office space as long as you have a laptop and an Internet connection.

- You can work for yourself and decide when you want to work. This enables you to spend more quality time with family and friends.
- Prevent brain drain that comes with mundane and monotonous daily office tasks.

## How much money can you potentially earn?

The earning capacity for anyone becoming a virtual assistant is unlimited and isn't hindered by the number of hours that you work with your client. This is because once your freelancing business grows, you can hire someone else to do the work for you and you keep a cut of the profit. In most cases, the top-earning virtual assistants usually have more clients and tasks than they can handle.

As a beginner into this industry, you'll need to start from scratch and slowly build up your credentials and portfolio with your respective clients. Once you acquire a good amount of reference and experience, you can start charging anywhere from $20 to $40 per hour based on your skill set and experience. Some experienced virtual assistants have even charged clients in excess of $50 to $100 per hour. However, it's important that you also ensure that the rates you'll be charging are not too exorbitant than the local pay rates when you are starting out at first.

## How it works - Step-by-Step

Many virtual assistants begin their paths by promoting themselves through sites such as Linkedin and Upwork. There are also sites that focus largely on virtual assistants like VAClassroom and agencies like Zirtual. However, before you embark on your journey into the virtual assistant world, you may want to consider the following steps:

- Never quit your 9-5 job right away when you initially begin. Always ensure that you have enough income saved for at least six or nine months for living expenses depending on your situation.

- Determine what tasks suit your prior experience or what you enjoy most doing. You may want to test your suitability and strengths for low-risk assignments first to determine what you would be good at.

- Open an account in a professional website. Highlight your skills and experience. Once you start getting jobs, add in testimonials and samples of your previous work to attract new clients.

## Myths about Virtual Training

Here are some common myths uncovered about working as a virtual assistant:

- **Virtual assistants are expensive -** The cost of hiring a virtual assistant can differ, depending on the kind of work that a client is seeking. If the client is looking for a niche or specific skill set, then he or she should be prepared to pay more. But if one is looking for someone to do just general clerical work, the costs will be much cheaper. On that note, it does save organizations money as you only need to pay these virtual assistants the cost for completing the work and excludes other benefits that they pay their normal staff such as year-end bonuses, medical claims, and so on.

- **Virtual assistants are always work-at-home moms -** Being a virtual assistant allows one to have the flexibility to work from anywhere; for parents, it enables them to work from home and spend more time with their children. However, not all who pursue this path are parents, since some are professionals who still work at their day jobs but use this opportunity to generate more income and others choose this career to travel and work from any location.

- **Virtual assistants are just online personal assistants** - It's be short -sighted to think of virtual assistants as just merely secretaries or personal assistants as they can perform a wide range of tasks that help a business. Here are some of the key roles that a virtual assistant performs:
    a. Creating social media content
    b. Sales support
    c. Email management
    d. Proofreading, writing, editing
    e. Web design
    f. Graphic design

## Idea #8 - Creating Online Courses

### What is it?

An online course is a platform in which an individual can provide information or tutorials on a vast array of subjects that he or she either has a passion for or experience. This can range for a variety of topics from culinary arts, music, software, fitness, gardening, and soon on. Contrary to popular belief, you don't have to be an expert in your field to come up with an online course. You just need to have more knowledge on the subject than most people. While some individuals have shared their knowledge through books, blogs, and online videos, creating an online course is a great method of generating passive income. Many people have made tons of money through their online courses over the years. According to global industry analysts, online learning will be a $240 billion dollar industry by the year 2021.

### Who is it for?

Creating an online course isn't limited just to the professional or experts in a given field. In our day-to-day life, we're already sharing our knowledge and information to those around us through daily conversations, our Instagram posts or Facebook feeds without even knowing about it. We reiterated that we all have knowledge in a certain area that someone else does not have and wants to learn. Are you already sharing your fitness regimes or travel recommendations on your social media accounts? Then it's probably high time you invest your time to combine all these details into an online course. A popular online learning platform called Udemy already has over 35,000 instructors offering 80,000 courses. As such, if you have a passion or knowledge in any areas of your life, you might want to consider applying into a course as you're probably already teaching others and not even aware of it.

## How much money can you potentially earn?

The average worker in the U.S makes an average of $25 per hour. With an online course, your income potential is unlimited. This happens, because after completing most of the initial work up front, you can continue to generate revenue every time you sell a course over the period of the next few months or even years. And the more courses you create and sell, your revenue keeps increasing.

## How does it work?

If you're thinking of diving into the world of selling online courses, you can follow the steps below to prepare yourself:

- Topic – First, you need to figure what you know or what you're passionate about. Try to think of subjects that you constantly help your friends and families on or even a hobby or sport that you've been doing for some time. Make a list of these things.

- Do Market Research - The next important step is to conduct market research on the topics that you have listed out in the earlier step. Here you'll need to determine if people would be willing to spend money on the topics that you will be teaching.

- Structuring The Outline Of Your Course - Prepare modules and lessons that will cover all important aspects of your course. These modules should dwell deeply into the subject matter and help the reader better understand the course.

- Teaching Method - Identify the best format that you will use for your online course. Will it be by text, audio, video or worksheets? Certain topics will require

*Passive Income Ideas*

only one format, while others will require two or three more formats to better convey the information.

- Drafting Your Lessons - When creating your online lessons, consider creating a visually appealing content that will attract the reader. Also, always proofread all texts and watch all videos to correct errors.

- How To Sell Your Lessons - For starters, you may want to opt for an easy alternative by using online platforms such as Skillshare or Udemy. You just upload the content of your lesson on these sites and then they'll take care of marketing these courses interested individuals.

- Keeping Course Information Up To Date - Every now and then, do a quick check to ensure that the content in your course is relevant with the current times. Continue to update and make changes to ensure that you don't receive any negative reviews that can derail the sale of your course.

## Myths about Creating Online Courses

It's imperative to note that while it may seem easy and cheap to start an online course, you must be aware that there are many other individuals who are also providing a similar course online. As such, you'll have to market your content aggressively, which will require time and money on your part.

# Idea #9 - Building an Application

## What is it?

In this day and age, almost every individual owns a smartphone. And with the usage of smartphones comes the usage of apps that are created by third-party developers on both the Android and iPhone platforms. Since apps have made their debut, it's estimated currently as a billion-dollar industry, and it doesn't seem to be slowing down anytime soon. Creating an app starts with an idea, and it'll also need to encompass some basic knowledge in coding.

## Who is it for?

Individuals who are already familiar with the basic coding language or have developed basic apps have a head start in this area. But for a non-coder that has an idea that would work, it's best to learn the required coding skills that will be important in creating an app of your choice. Kevin Systrom, the founder of Instagram, learned coding at night to build Burbn, which in time turned to Instagram and was sold to Facebook for an estimated value of $1 billion.

## How much money can you potentially earn?

It is estimated that in 2016, the revenue generated from apps is somewhere in the region of $46 billion. A large chunk of this revenue comes from mobile app games. For the iOS platform, it is estimated that 25% of the developers earn anywhere between $5,000 per month and about 18% of developers on the Android platform earn the same number. There are multiple ways to earn revenue through the apps on both these platforms. They are:

    a. Provide a free version of your app but charge a certain amount for the premium version.

*Passive Income Ideas*

    b. Allow ads to be displayed in your ads to generate income.

    c. Collect and sell data to organizations that require info for their businesses.

## How It Works - Step-by-Step

Once you have devised an idea for an app and some basic coding knowledge, you can follow these steps to create your first app.

1. Set A Goal For Your App - Using a pen and paper, ask the following questions:

    a. What exactly do you want your app to do?

    b. How are you going to make it appeal to users?

    c. What problem is it going to solve?

    d. How will you market your app?

2. Turn Your Ideas Into Sketches

    a. With the answers from Step 1, create visual representations of your thoughts into what your app will look like.

    b. Make decisions if you're going to include ads to generate revenue or will your app be a paid download.

    c. Sketch as many ideas as possible.

3. Market Research

    a. Research your competition to make your app better

    b. Read the competition's reviews.

    c. Make changes to your ideas and sketches to make necessary changes based on the info collected.

d. Determine your target market and how will you market your idea.

   e. Look for new and refreshing designs for your app.

4. Creating A Wireframe

   a. Now, you'll take all the ideas and sketches and provide them with more contexts.

   b. Using a wireframing website, you can start to put some functionality to your ideas in your app.

5. Designing Your App's Back End

   a. Once the wireframe has been constructed, you'll need to delineate your servers, APIs, and data diagrams.

   b. For the novice, you can source the web for app builders that will provide you the necessary tools for this.

6. Get Feedback

   a. Give a demonstration of your app to your family and friends. Get their feedback on areas to improve.

   b. Their feedback will be crucial in finalizing the overall structure of your app and functionality.

7. Putting The Pieces Together

   a. Once you have gone through the above process, you can start finalizing your app using your app builder.

   b. Now is the time to create an account with Google Play and Apple, so that you can create your app on the market

c. At this stage, you may want to engage designers to create your user interface for your app.

8. App Testing
   a. At this stage, it is important to test both the functionality and user interface of your app.
   b. You can use platforms like Proto and Pixate to test your app.
   c. Make any changes and adjustments to your app based on the test results before moving on to the beta testing phase.
   d. During the beta testing phase, you may use both Android and iOS platforms to test the app in a live environment.

9. Releasing Your App
   a. You can now start adding your app into both the Android and iOS stores.
   b. For the Google Play store, you will be immediately selling your app.
   c. For the iOS store, it will be reviewed first before it goes live.

**Myths about Building an Application**
- Mobile Apps Are Cheap - Development of simple apps are by no means cheap as there is extensive effort and time that goes in the development of these applications.
- Apps Are Usually Aimed At Smartphones - While the largest users of mobile applications are individuals with smartphones, mobile apps can also be used for tablets, handheld consoles, and smartwatches.

# Idea #10 - Online Auctions

## What it is?

Another popular method of generating passive income is through the use of online auctions. Using this platform to generate revenue is fast becoming a favorite, as it's relatively simple compared to the work that you would put in. To do this, you would just need to create an online profile and begin to sell your merchandise to interested individuals. Plus, in recent times, users are quick to use the drop shipping options that are offered by many companies. You become the middleman by displaying the goods from the supplier on the online platform and once it's purchased by the interested party, the goods are directly shipped from the manufacturer to them. Hence, you make the money without the need of keeping inventory.

## Who is it for?

The best thing about using this method to generate revenue is that it can be done by anyone with a laptop and an internet connection. Anyone that has either goods or craft items to sell can utilize this method. Plus, you can also purchase highly sought items from manufacturers and resell them on these websites or through an auction.

## How it works - Step-by-Step

The first key step in generating revenue from an online auction is to research, research, and research. You don't want to sell stuff where there isn't any demand; hence, it is vital that you look for goods that are highly sought after and can be sold at a premium.

The next step in generating revenue and increasing your profit margin is to find out the starting bid price for your item. The trick here is to determine how popular the item that you will be placing for the bid is. If a certain product is

*Passive Income Ideas*

high in demand, you can start the bid at a low price. But if there aren't going to be many bidders for a particular item, then you should go with a price close enough to the actual price of the item.

Next, to attract the attention of potential bidders, you will need to come up with a catchy phrase for your listing. And it'll also help to give a little description of the product so that potential bidders will be more open to placing a bid for it. Also, to ensure success to your online auction, you'll need to ensure that each product is listed in the right category to verify that you only attract the right bidders who will be more prone to purchasing your items.

When you start, your auctions will also have an effect on its success and failures. It's recommended that you begin your auction on Thursdays and have them run for ten days straight. This will allow your auction to be open for two weekends straight. This will ensure more traffic time to your auction site.

## Myths about Online Auctions

Here are some points to dispel the typical myths associated with online auctions:

- Items will not fetch their fair market value - Those who usually buy items online are pretty seasoned buyers and will have probably done their homework in terms of the price of that specific item. As such, they will normally purchase these items at their fair prices.
- Selling with an online auction platform is expensive - Contrary to popular belief, there are many online platforms that are willing to negotiate on the commission rates that are reasonable depending on the item that you are selling.
- Auctions only attract buyers looking for a bargain - Not all online buyers are bargain hunters. Many of

them are always on the lookout for items that are considered collectibles and hard to find. As such, if you have these kinds of items, you'll surely attract serious buyers.

# Idea #11 - Online Survey

## What it is?

An online survey is a set of questionnaires for an individual to complete on the web. These surveys are a set of questions that are created using a web form that is eventually connected to a database that will store all responses which, in turn, will be used as a statistic for further analysis. Many organizations employ these online surveys to gain a better understanding of their target customers. The feedback provided by respondents in these surveys will help organizations improve their products and services. Surveys serve two distinct functions; one is to collect more data on the demographics of the customer base. The other is to gather feedback on a certain type of product or service provided by the organization. Online surveys are widely used these days as opposed to traditional surveys as there is a much broader outreach to respondents at both local and international stage. Most organizations usually will provide cash incentives to individuals to participate in their surveys.

## Who is it for?

In online surveys, the organization is looking for individuals that fit into the character of their sample. As such, when you register to an online survey platform, you'll first need to undergo a pre-qualification test. From here, these platforms will start sending your surveys based on the demographic that you qualify into. So, if you have plenty of spare time on your hands, you should first sign up to as many online surveys websites as possible to expedite.

## How much money can you potentially earn?

- Vindale – One of the best survey companies in relation to pay and time spent. Between $150 - $200 a month.

- Earning Station – Between $120 - $180 per month
- PineCone – minimum $3 for per survey
- Paribus – Between $70 - $100 per month
- My Survey – Between $150 - $200 per month

The major benefit is that you can take these surveys during your free time while watching a movie, having a meal at home, yet still earning a substantial amount.

## How it works - Step-by-Step

To help you in generating income from online surveys, we recommend the following steps:

1. Register as many free online survey companies as you can. The more you join, the more surveys will be sent to your email and more revenue you will be able to generate.
2. Do not lie when you register on these online survey sites.
3. Always keep your profile updated to eventually allow more surveys to be sent to you.
4. Read and answer all questions carefully. Every survey has qualifying and quality questions to ensure that the respondent is giving this or her honest answers.
5. Each survey has a designated time frame to complete it. As such, do not rush, but instead, take your time and answer each question after reading it thoroughly and carefully.
6. Do not take multiple surveys all at once. Complete one at a time. Since some surveys have a limited timeframe, completing multiple surveys at one go may prevent you from completing a survey within the allotted time frame.

7. Always ensure that you complete the survey at one go. Most surveys are only available for a certain period of time only. Once a predetermined number of surveys are collected, the survey is no longer available. Hence, it's vital to complete a survey from start to finish at once.

## **Myths**

Online surveys are an excellent way for many people to make some extra money on the side. In turn, an influx of people have signed up to participate in online surveys, which has perpetuated a number of myths. Here are some typical examples:

- nline survey sites are nothing more than a scam – Contrary to popular belief, there are more legitimate sites than scams when it comes to online surveys. Legitimate sites are free to join and they will not ask you to pay anything upfront and most legitimate sites use PayPal as a means for payment transactions.

- Online survey sites only hire experienced individuals – Not true. Anyone can qualify for a survey and experience is not a means for qualification.

- It only takes a few minutes to answer a survey – Most surveys will take some time for you to complete them properly. Remember, answer honestly as you risk losing your account if you just barge your way through the survey.

- Online surveys are a get rich quick scheme – No, don't go and quit your day job over online surveys. Online surveys help to provide a supplementary income stream and it is by no means can get you rich overnight. To generate more revenue, it's best to register with as many online survey companies and participate in as many surveys as possible.

# Idea #12 - Online Consultancy

## What it is?

nline consultancy is a highly broad terminology, and it covers a huge number of topics and roles. The need for online consultancy usually stems from market demand. Some of the fields that usually require online consultancy are:

- Accounting
- Advertising
- Auditing
- Business
- Business writing
- Career counseling
- Communications
- Computer consulting
- Editorial services
- Headhunting

Organizations often seek online consultants due to these primary reasons:

- Consultant's experience and expertise
- A different outlook and solutions to the issues being faced by the organization
- The temporary overhead for a short period of time

## Who is it for?

Honestly, everyone with a decent knowledge on a particular topic can become a consultant on it. In short, you really don't have to be an expert with many years of experience. But you shouldn't resort to unethical practices when providing your knowledge and insight on a particular field or topic.

## How much money can you potentially earn?

These top online consulting sites below demonstrate the range of typical online consultancy charges for their services:

- Clarity – a minimum hourly rate of $60. A site for upcoming entrepreneurs and consultants are usually seasoned experts.
- Maven Research, Inc – a minimum hourly rate of $25. Consultants for a variety of subjects.

In 2013, the market size for online consulting was estimated at around 39.3 billion, and it shows no sign of slowing down presently. In 2013, 42% of organizations planned to hire more online consultants and another 5% planned to increase their budget to spend on online consultants.

## How it works - Step-by-Step

In becoming an online consultant, you're required to provide feedback and advice to individuals or companies that may range from a broad range of topics or a particular niche subject. If you desire to become an online consultant, you may follow the steps below to launch:

1. Identify your niche – You'll not only want to define in what areas that you have the knowledge and experience that can be beneficial as a consultant but also an area of particular interest.
2. If required, get the proper certification and licenses – do some research and find out if any formal licenses or certification is required for your field of interest before going online as a consultant (i.e. accounting).

You'll also need to check local licenses and regulations that are required before embarking on this path.

3. Have patience – Every business takes time to grow. If you lack the patience in growing the business, you'll be doomed to fail. Thus, it's essential for you to establish your long term and short-term goals.

4. Identify your target market – Please ensure the area of your intended consultancy has ample demand and is profitable. Otherwise, your business is set up for failure.

5. Research – As in all businesses, you will need to do massive amounts of research. From identifying your target market, scoping out your competition, how you will market your services and how will you help your potential customers.

## **Myths**

Here are some common myths usually associated with online consulting:

- It's expensive – Getting started with online consulting is relatively inexpensive. All you need is a laptop an internet connection and you're good to go.
- No personal touch – A large part of online consulting requires one to be good at selling yourself as well as the services you provide. And not to mention, you'll need to be in touch with your customers regularly to meet their requirements.
- You need to be an expert – This myth is relatively untrue; however, you'll need to pair the knowledge and experience you have together with something that you're passionate about to truly stand out as an online consultant.

## Idea #13 – Cryptocurrency

### What is it?

Cryptocurrency is a digital currency that, as the name suggests, that uses cryptography for security purposes. In sum, a cryptocurrency is very difficult to duplicate. The basis of cryptocurrencies is based on what is known as a blockchain, which is a distributed ledger connected by a large network of computers. Cryptocurrency has one unique feature. It's uncontrolled by any central banking authority of any country. At present, there are many cryptocurrencies in circulation and one of the most popular ones is Bitcoin.

Cryptocurrencies enable payments that are made online to be secure and are usually referred to as "tokens.. Various encryption algorithms are used when cryptocurrencies are used for secure payments online.

### Who is it for?

or starters, starting with cryptocurrencies can be a little tricky as there is a lot of jargon that you'll need to understand in order to make a profit from this. In a nutshell, if you have some substantial amount of cash that you would like to invest in cryptocurrencies without the fear of making losses, then, by all means, this is for you. But, if you prefer to have your money placed in more conventional investment methods, then stay clear of cryptocurrencies.

### How much money can you potentially earn?

Cryptocurrency has been the craze over the last few years, and its value is ever increasing. In 2017, Bitcoin went from $750 to $10,000 by the end of the year. If you would have invested about $10,000 of your savings into Bitcoin in January 2017, you would have received returns up to

$133,333 by December 2017. The total market value for all cryptocurrencies was valued at $500 billion at the end of 2017.

## How it works - Step-by-Step

Before diving into cryptocurrencies, it's important to consider several factors below:

1. Which cryptocurrency will be suitable for you? Specifically, consider how long it has been in the market, its market share, and also its purpose.
2. What type of investment will you be into? You need to determine the duration of your investment. Is it going to be short-term or long-term?
3. Research – Study the market and patterns of cryptocurrencies to determine if you'll be in it for the short or long term
4. Determine the amount of money you will invest – Always ensure you only invest what you are willing to lose. Don't go dive head in and put all your eggs in one basket in hopes of making a quick fortune.

## Myths about Cryptocurrency

Here are some myths regularly associated with cryptocurrencies:

- Cryptocurrencies are mostly used by criminals – The security features in cryptocurrencies negate this myth, thus making it totally secure.
- Cryptocurrencies can be shut down by the government – Not true. Unless the entire Internet decides to come crashing down, no government entity can shut down cryptocurrencies.

- Cryptocurrencies are illegal – While some countries like Russia have banned the usage of cryptocurrencies like Bitcoin, many others have encouraged the usage of cryptocurrencies as a means of a payment transaction.

# Idea #14 - Make YouTube Videos

## What is Youtube?

How many videos have you watched today? Chances are an average of 5? Or maybe 3? If by now you don't know what YouTube is, you're probably not one of those people who are always on online. YouTube, simply put, is a video sharing platform. Sustain all contractions No matter the number, you know that video content makes the arsenal of content marketing. It was the success of many campaigns in 2018 and it will likely continue in 2019. YouTube is an essential tool for plenty of industries. Even before YouTube, brands and companies have been creating videos to showcase their products and services: and now with YouTube, it makes it much easier for both brands and individuals to create and upload videos.

## Who is YouTube for?

To answer this question, you need to ask yourself a series of questions. Firstly- do you have visual content? Is your brand, company, or product something your target audience can see, touch, hold, or hear? What industry are you in and what is your target audience? Are they 65-year olds and above? Are they toddlers? Are they fathers who have daughters? The kinds of videos there are on YouTube are of different types from how-tos to DIY to tutorials to promo materials to information, edutainment, interviews, and so on. Answering the questions above can ultimately help you decide whether or not you should be on YouTube.

## How much money can you potentially earn from YouTube?

n Youtube, consistency is crucial if your main aim is to grow your channel. Much like blogging, the more consistent you are at posting content on your channel, the higher the

*Passive Income Ideas*

probability of reaching a wider audience. A strict publishing schedule is what most YouTubers stick with - they post at least one video each week on a specific day. The truth is, anyone can upload a video but not everyone can make a fortune out of it. To give you an idea, SuperWoman Lilly Singh raked in $10.5 million in 2017. Daniel Middleton earned $16.5 million through YouTube videos and Logan Paul made $12.5 million.

**How does YouTube Work?**

The steps for using YouTube are quite simple:

Step 1- Start by watching YouTube videos either anonymously or by logging into your Google or Facebook account. Get a feel of the types of videos on YouTube.

Step 2- Get an Account to Broadcast Yourself or your brand

Step 3- Use YouTube for basic activities such as liking and commenting

Step 4- Browse and watch YouTube videos

Step 5- Craft and create your own videos

Step 6- Upload your videos

However, there's more to it than that if you want to use YouTube to make money. You need to optimize your video content in order to establish your YouTube channel. Before you get started on creating videos, take the time to do your research on keywords as well as video content so you can create a video that fits these keywords for the audience you want to target.

- Make Compelling Titles - Your video can be so awesome but without a title to hook a viewer, nobody is going to click on it. Having a killer title is so important because this is the first time a viewer will see.

- Create Perfect YouTube Thumbnails- The second most important thing viewers look at is your thumbnail. The right kind of thumbnail will attract a reader to click on it, making your video trend as well as make your channel recognizable. Just like the title, your thumbnail should be relevant to the content as well as correspond with your video title. Attractive thumbnails result in higher clicks. Also, include short descriptions in your thumbnail, so viewers can understand what your video features.

- Limit Videos to no more than 10 Minutes - The total watch time of your videos is also crucial. Long videos that have content repeating itself will not help. So if your videos are longer than 10 minutes, you need to ensure that it gives a good enough reason for your viewers to want to continue being interested in your videos. However, it is a great idea to make the video just over 10 minutes long, because once it goes over 10 minutes, you can place more ads in the video and significantly increase your ad revenue.

- Brand Your YouTube Channel - Let's face it, YouTube viewers and channels are so sophisticated now that there is no way you can get away with not having a consistent image for your channel. If YouTube is going to make a big part of your marketing arsenal, then you'd better brand it, so it's consistent with your other platforms and digital spaces. You need to make it visually attractive to not only encourage your visitors to take your brand seriously but also want to brand it so that it's cohesive and delivers the same consistent marketing message across all platforms - both online and offline. Branding also increases brand recall and awareness.

- Include Calls-to-Action (CTAs) - Adding calls-to-action to your videos will help you create more engagement on YouTube. They can also be irritating, so try to use them in the right way. No matter what goals you have, to get more likes or more subscribers, be clear and concise about key actions people need to take.

- Share Videos via Social Media -To grow your channel, sharing is important, whether you share on your social channels or people share your videos. You need to publish your latest videos on your other platforms as well as engage and stay active on your social communities and groups. Each social platform has its own distinctive culture. As a savvy marketer, it's your job to find out what this distinction is and use it to your advantage.

## Myths about Youtube

- ou get paid based on the subscribers you have.

  Not true. Subscriber counts have no bearings where Google Adsense is concerned. The mechanics here is that YouTubers get paid for the amount of pre-roll ads that are viewed each time their video is seen, which if you look at it, the more views a person gets on their video means the more people will click on ads. From that perspective, subscriber numbers are imperative, but it doesn't mean that YouTubers get paid per subscriber.

- No violent or provocative videos are allowed.

  Pornography, abusive hate speech, nudity as well as dead bodies are all rightly banned, but there is still a multitude of other inappropriate content on YouTube from gun violence to car accidents and the like. While YouTube's community guidelines talk about the kinds of content that should be posted, the enforcement is not hard enough.

- Short videos get more views

The type of video you post needs to be adequately long so that viewers know what you want them to see and that they get the information they want in good timing. Attention spans get shorter as time goes by and content can be attained at a rapid pace, however, short videos only work for the certain time of content such as those that are fun, fast, and entertaining. Videos such as how-tos, recipes, and even Ted Talks and debates can take longer than 5 minutes. What you don't want in your videos is FLUFF. Too much of unnecessary commenting and talking or too much of fancy video design can dull the mind.

## Idea #15 - Online Fitness Instructor

### What is an Online Fitness Instructor?

An online personal trainer is an occupation that allows you to take your fitness training offline to online. Via this way, you get to reach more clients who want to be inspired and have fitness content right on their mobile phones. Becoming an online fitness instructor also means that you can dramatically increase your income because you can train your regular clients face-to-face and also acquire an online following of clients who are anywhere in the world. Becoming an online fitness instructor allows you to make a living out of doing what you love, and it also enables clients to search for a trainer who best fits clients' fitness goals.

### Who is it for?

Are you a fitness professional who loves training clients? Are you active on social and digital media? If you love training clients, motivating them to become better versions of themselves, and sharing your fitness routines and exercises, then this route to earn more and experience financial freedom is for you!

It helps if you have a certificate as this would give credibility to your skill set because if you are calling yourself an instructor, then a certificate would definitely give you an edge.

### How much money can you potentially earn?

In most cases, the area you live in decides the factor of how easily you can earn as a fitness instructor. With online coaching though, borders are not an issue because you can reach a wider and more niche audience with your style and brand of fitness. Fitness instructors typically charge about $50 to $100 per hour for training sessions. To become an online fitness instructor, you need to create your own program and keep posting videos, content and other material to keep your clients informed of the plan, the level of commitment, as well as meal plans that come with it.

You can do this via asking them to subscribe to your mailing list where you can send them instructional videos and meals plans on a daily or weekly basis based on the plan that they have subscribed and paid for. You can earn an average of $200 a week to $500 a month. The stronger the following you have on the online space, the better your chances of improving your bank balance.

## How to become an online fitness instructor?

There is no one-size-fits-all step-by-step guide in becoming an online fitness instructor because it depends on your brand of fitness. Some instructors focus on muscle gain for competition, some focus on lean bodies with good mobility, some instructors focus on HIIT workouts only, some instructors include martial arts into training, some focus on making you a better runner or ballerina or swimmer, while some focus on yoga or Pilates. As a result, there are guidelines you can use as a compass to help you get started:.

## Step 1 Find Your Niche

As there are many types of fitness exercises out there, identifying your fitness niche is crucial so you can target the kind of audience who are looking for your brand of fitness be it HIIT, cardio kickboxing, yoga, bodyweight exercises, running, and so on.

## Step 2 Determine your USP

Your unique selling proposition tells people why you and your fitness brand are unique. You may offer an exceptional type of fitness that is ideal for people who have little time on their hands to exercise or your brand of fitness may be perfect for postpartum mothers. Whatever it is, identify your USP because it'll help you get the right audience.

### Step 3 Choose your Promotional Channels

In today's visually-charged world, certain platforms work exceptionally well as promotional channels for fitness. Tumblr was one of the channels used back before Instagram exploded on the scene and made video sharing workouts easily accessible. YouTube is also another way to get your programs available to your clients.

### Step 4 Work on your clients

One of the ways Kayla Itsines's fitness programs is immensely popular is because her fitness program thrives on a community of positivity and geared towards health instead of achieving the perfect body. She also encourages her clients who do her workouts through her Sweat App to take before and after images showing the progress of their bodies. When it comes to your online fitness program, think about how to invest in your clients because they are the best form of marketing and publicity for you.

### Myths about Online Fitness Instructors

- Fitness Instructors earn plenty because they have celebrity clients

  The moniker "Celebrity" Trainer is used when the trainer has clients who work in the public eye. While it's great to have a celebrity as a client, not all clients of a fitness instructor are celebrities and not all fitness instructors have celebrity clients. Some have none. Though having a celebrity client helps, the instructor doesn't rely solely on the celebrity client, so one's means of earning has to be varied, so that income is continuous. Most personal trainers make most of their living on average non-public eye clients.

- Fitness trainers love being in their workout clothes

  When we see an online fitness trainer, we always view them through the videos or photos they post on their blog or on social media and they are always in workout clothes simply because you observe them when they are working out. But like anyone else, fitness instructors also look forward to dressing up and wearing other kinds of clothing.

- Fitness trainers can also give you specific eating and meal plans as well as the right supplements

  Most fitness trainers provide advice on what to eat it and how much as a recommendation, but they don't offer specific eating plans because this is outside their practice. This also relates to medication and supplements. The trainer always aims to education, but if a client wants to take a supplement, specific advice should come from a doctor.

## Idea #16 - Renting out space via AirBnB

### What is AirBnB?

If you have a spare room that you're not using, you are sitting on potential income. Did you know that? Your home is your asset and if you can monetize from it, it can defray some of your living costs. It could also potentially fix the problem of having a house too big for the upkeep.

AirBnB is an online avenue which allows people to rent out their spaces, spare rooms, or properties to guests. When space is rented, AirBnB takes 3 percent of the commission from every book from a host and 6 to 12 percent from guests. You can have different kinds of one-of-a-kind property on AirBnB from shared rooms to boutique treehouses, an entire house with different kinds of amenities.

### Who is it for?

AirBnB is for anyone looking to make extra money from their living spaces and property. It's perfect for people who have a large house but would like extra money for the upkeep or those who like managing properties for homestays and unique accommodations but without the huge costs that come with purchasing and managing conventional properties such as hotels.

### How much money can you potentially earn through AirBnB?

AirBnB, since its inception, has enabled more than 160 million guests to find the right accommodations through more than 3 million listings all around the world. According to Priceonomicthis, AirBnB hosts earn more than anyone else in the gig economy, with the average earnings at $924 a month. However, take note that earnings range depending on the property as well as the location. Some hosts even make more than $10,000 a month, while some make less than $500 a month.

## How does AirBnB work?

Step 1 - Firstly, you need to own a space to rent whether a room, an apartment, or a house.

Step 2 - Next, you must register your listing on AirBnB and give them the specifications of your property such as the size, its area, number of rooms, and other details requested by AirBnB. You'll also need to open a host profile with a picture of yourself and go through scanning and verification processes.

Step 3 - You'll also need to check out the legality of listing out your space in your neighborhood or city because some areas have various laws on renting out spaces in a home for a certain period of time. So make sure to check your local laws concerning renting your home.

Step 4 - Once you have your profile ready and your information verified, you can continue with listing your spaces at the 'List Your Space' section. Here, you can describe the kind of lodging you plan on listing and information such as location, how many guests you can accommodate as well as the availability of your property. You can also set your price per night, per week, or by month.

Step 5 - List your property as best as you can and this also means posting high-quality photos of your listing, so customers will have a good idea of how the property looks like, how big it is, and if it suits their needs.

Once your listing is all set up, you'll be given AirBnB's variety of services such as Host Guarantee, insurance programs as well first aid kids and refunds. AirBnB also handles the payments. Payment options depend greatly on a country and can be paid through PayPal, wire transfer, or direct deposit.

## Myths about AirBnB

- **Increased Wear and Tear -** The biggest myth going around is that your home, your room, or whatever property you rent out will be severely damaged. Yes, you've probably read news about how some property has been damaged but fret not, AirBnB offers insurance coverage for all property rented through AirBnB.

  However, the likelihood of a guest damaging your property is low because most people don't damage the place where they stay due to respect.

  With every business, there is a risk but the last thing you want to worry about is your property damage. Yes, there would be wear and tear but that is part of maintaining your space.

- **Tourism changing the locality -** It seems like a bad idea if an influx of travelers coming to your community, but tourism also brings diversity and opens the opportunity for new ideas as well as new income not just for hosts but also for the people in the community. AirBnB offers travelers and hosts alike a unique experience. Instead of huge hotels taking over both space and economy of the local community, hosting travelers with existing property enables the existing businesses to thrive.

- **You will end up with party-goers -** One of the main concerns of AirBnB hosts is the few bad apples that we read in the news. Yes, AirBnB homes are perfect for party and gatherings and out of 80,000 bookings per day, only on rare occasions would you read issues of a host's homes being irresponsibly used as party venues and guests not taking the responsibility to clean up or make good of the property.

# Idea #17 - Becoming a Silent Partner

**What it a Silent Partner?**

A silent business partner is a person who contributes to a business financially but does not contribute any other ways such as in the day-to-day running of the business. The primary reason or motivation of being a silent partner is the return on investment. Silent partners want profits from owning a business, but they don't want to be involved in the actual management of the company.

While it's easy to assume that a silent partner's responsibility is only to provide the financial capacity of business, silent partners can also contribute to other tasks such as:

- Giving additional capital when a business is low in funds
- Offering the collateral needed to qualify for a loan
- Making connections to ensure business growth

**Who is it for?**

As a silent partner, you have the ability to earn a return of money when the business makes a profit. This is an ideal form of passive income for people who want to make money and own a business but don't want to be involved in the day-to-day running of the business. The amount of income you make will depend entirely on how well the business is doing and the arrangements you've made with the other partners. For instance, some silent partners take home a smaller share of profits than the active partner, and it also depends on the amount invested in it.

It's also perfect for people who have money but do not want to be involved in too many businesses and lessen the hassle and stress of running multiple projects.

## How much money can you potentially earn?

For the initial investment made, silent partners will often receive stock in the company as well as a set percentage of the profits. The amount of passive income earned also depends on how well the company performs and the agreements made as part of the silent partner contract. More often than not, the silent partner earns a much smaller share of the revenue compared to active partners.

When it comes to losses and debts, all partners, silent or active, are responsible for the finances of the business; however, thanks to limited liability, silent business partners are generally liable for the amount or percentage that they invested in the business when it was formed. For example, a partner who has invested 15% in the business is only responsible for 15% of the losses and debts. The percentage, details, and agreement of the partnership must be decided at the initiation of the business to avoid any misunderstandings and legal disputes. Both the partners and the owners of the business must acknowledge each investment for tax purposes.

## How to become a silent partner?

If you like the idea of becoming a silent partner, here is how you can do it:

**Step 1** - To become a silent partner, you can do so by entering into a limited partnership agreement with a start-up or business owner. The other person is an active partner and this partner will be responsible for the daily business. Your participation in this is limited or essentially silent and the only thing you need to worry about it having money to be pumped into the business as and when needed.

**Step 2** - When you enter into a limited partnership, you need a written partnership agreement drawn and all partners involved must agree to the terms of the contract.

Step 3 - You need to formally register your limited partnership with your local clerk where the business is located as well as with the Secretary of State. Silent and active partners are both obligated to be held liable for the business debts unless a form of limited liability partnership or LLP is formed. With the LLP, general partners will be responsible for business debts.

**Step 4** - Once your partnership has been registered, you must next apply for an EIN or Employer Identification Number. This number allows you to pay your business taxes and also enables you open a business bank account for the funds for your partnership.

*Passive Income Ideas*

# Idea #18- Cashback Rewards with Credit Cards

## What is cashback rewards with credit cards?

Cashback rewards deliver an easy way of getting a little money with every purchase you make with your credit card, which is why it makes them appealing to customers. The main benefit of Cashback cards is the simplicity of how it works. When it comes to redemption, Cashback credit cards are pretty straightforward, and users do not need to think too much about how much they are earning. Most people usually just deduct their Cashback from their statement balance or just redeem their points via gift cards. Cashback cards come in a variety of options from bonus category, flat percentage Cashback cards as well as bonus category. Whatever the mechanism, all of them pay you back.

## Who is it for?

It's ideal for people who want to make some money especially if they use their credit card plenty of times and for very big purchases such as airline tickets, cab fare, and groceries.

## How much money can you potentially earn?

When you live on a fixed income, an option to make extra money helps. For example, you can use your Bank of America Cash Reward Card to bump up your bottom line. If you receive a $150 initial cash bonus after getting your card, you can earn at least 1 percent on all purchases you make via the card. Depending on the purchases as well, you get 2 percent if you get groceries or 3 percent on gas. What you get from your card enables you to purchase other things. If you're mindful of what you spend on, you can make Cashback worth up to $300 a year.

## How do cashback rewards work?

Cashback is essentially a rebate of the purchases you make using your card. Card issues can afford a Cashback program because their merchants pay an interchange fee for every transaction made. For example, if you pay a merchant $100 using your credit card, then the merchant will only receive $97. A TV that you pay for $700 would give you a $14 net and a 2 percent Cashback card. And the merchant would need to pay a transaction fee of $21 since you used your card.

If it's a flat-rate Cashback program, every purchase you make earns the same percentage Cashback.

If it is the bonus cards and tiered cards program, then you earn different percentages depending on the category which means you earn a little bit more Cashback.

Merchants will know what type of spending qualifies for a percentage as there are merchant category codes that are four-digit numbers that specify the business type. These codes are used by credit card networks to categorize and track purchases.

## Myths about Credit Card Cashback Programs

- **Applying for credit cards will hurt a person's credit score**

The only thing that will hurt your credit score is if you don't make your payments in time. Applying for a single credit card and making your payments in due time will make your credit score on the positive side. A credit card is worth applying for so long as you know your spending limits and spend wisely.

- **Canceling credit cards will definitely help my score**

Canceling credit cards will actually hurt your credit score because it'll reduce the total amount of credit you have been extended and it will also increase your debt-to-credit ratio. Canceling cards because you are afraid you'll go over the spending limit will also reduce your average length of credit card history. As long as you're not paying unreasonable annual fees, then it's wise to keep your existing cards on a good credit report.

- **Earning points and miles is not worth it**

One of the biggest reasons to use a credit card is to accumulate miles points. While it's true that airlines have limited availability of their awards seats at the lowest mileage levels and hotels try their hardest to hide blackout dates, it is still value for people who are willing to look hard enough for rewards. You can still sit on business class seats if you are flexible on dates and book your flights well in advance. Last minute flights can also give you great value when you compare it to walk-up and full-fare prices.

If you do your research properly, you'll find plenty of awards that you can use and book over the phone. Also, there are plenty of programs out there that offer awards with no blackout dates or even capacity controls, such as hotels from Starwood group as well as Southwest Airlines.

# Idea #19 - Renting Out Your Parking Spot

## What is it?

Got an empty parking space that's going to waste because you're not using it? Well, guess what? It's about to become yet another source of your passive income. If you live in an apartment that comes with two parking spaces and you've only got one car, this passive income option could definitely work for you. Or just about anyone with an extra parking spot to spare, really. Even better if this parking space happens to be near an event venue because you'll never be short of customers looking for the nearest parking available. You'd be surprised at how much some people would be willing to pay for convenience.

If you've ever wondered whether a parking spot could make a good investment in terms of generating passive income, the good news is *yes, they can*. In fact, just like real estate, a parking space is an investment that could potentially appreciate in its value over time while generating a steady cash flow stream for you every month (depending on where your parking spot is located of course).

## How much you could potentially earn?

Passive income rates and how much you could potentially earn with this option would depend on several factors. The closer or more conveniently located your parking spot is, the higher you'll be able to charge. If your parking spot is highly desirable, for example, if it's near public transportation, in a high-security location, or covered car park, for example, you'd certainly be able to charge much more than if your car park was just located in an open air area.

Parking rates would also depend on the city that you're located in. Prime cities like San Francisco and New York, for example, have the potential to charge much more if the parking spot is located in a premium location. Parking spaces

*Passive Income Ideas*

in this city can sometimes sell anywhere from $80,000 and more, especially if it's a standard parking spot located within a garage. Diving a little deeper into the San Francisco area, prime locations like Nob Hill or Russian Hill, for example, have parking spots which go for anywhere from $300 to $400 a month to rent. Depending on the needs of the customer you're dealing with, if one is looking to rent your parking spot long-term, there's the potential for long-term rental too, which means a consistent stream of income coming in each month. Even if you were to charge $5 per day for parking, you're still making an extra $150 a month.

**How does it work?**

Among the benefits of venturing into the parking lot rental business as a passive income option include that this is one of lower-risk "business" models that you could think about getting involved in. You don't need a lot of capital to get started if you do want to purchase a parking lot to start renting, and if you've already got a spare spot to spare, you don't even have to fork out any capital of your own at all! Another benefit is that this option doesn't require a lot of your time. You don't need to be there constantly having to manage or keep an eye on your parking spot. This is one of the few passive income options that just "sits there" and makes money for you without you having to do much at all. It's easy to get started renting out your parking spot. Here's how you get begin:

- Step 1: Start by advertising your parking spot online or on apps like BestParking, Spacer, Streetline, SpotHero, and more. Get the word out there that you've got a spot available for rent.
- Step 2: Check if your space can be used legally without a permit. If you need a permit, look into getting one before you attempt to rent your spot.

- Step 3: If you're renting an apartment with an extra parking spot, have a chat with your landlord to make sure they are comfortable with the arrangement.
- Step 4: Prepare a legal contract which clearly outlines the terms of agreements between you and the person who is renting out your parking spot.
- Step 5: Do a quick check to make sure if you're liable for taxes.

**Myths about Renting Your Parking Spot**

While there are no concrete myths about renting out your parking spaces, there are misconceptions that people will not be willing to pay to rent a spot to park. That's not entirely true; and in fact, if your rental charges are much cheaper than the rates that the city or town council would charge them, they'd be more than happy to come to you at the end of the day. Price it right and you'll have no problems finding renters and get your passive income going with this option.

## Idea #20 - Network Marketing

**What is it?**

Would you like to be paid continuously for work that you would only need to do once? Who wouldn't, right? However, very few businesses these days actually afford us that kind of opportunity. If you're lucky enough to be blessed with the gift of being able to sing or write, singers and authors are great examples of individuals who get paid repeatedly for a job they've done once. This is known as *royalty pay,* and each time that their song gets played or their book gets published, they get paid a royalty or a commission for it.

Now, for those of us who haven't been blessed with these talented gifts, there's another option you can consider as an alternative to generating some passive income for yourself. *Network marketing,* and before you're quick to dismiss this idea as nothing more than a scam, stop for a minute and consider the possibilities.

Network marketing works on the principle that you will continue to earn an income based on the effort that you had to invest in the initial stages. Since network marketing usually involves products and services, your income is going to be based on the sale of these said products and services. In fact, network marketing has quickly become a very popular option among those who are seeking flexibility while making a little bit of part-time income in addition to their full-time jobs.

Commonly referred to as multi-level marketing, this passive income approach uses the method of selling products via teamwork through a tiered structure comprising of sales associates. Making money depends on two things, which are your ability to sell and your ability to bring in new employees. While this tiered approach works well and can generate a fair bit of profit for the early participants and the original promoter, those who jump into the game may find it more challenging to see a turn of profit as quickly.

The reason why many are so quick to dismiss network marketing as a scam is because they're selling the *wrong* kind of products. What you want to aim for is *consumable products,* which are the most effective approach to take with network marketing for one very simple reason. These products are a necessity, they are consumed quickly and customers constantly need to replace these products repeatedly each time they run out of their own supply. When you pick the right products, the sales start to happen, and you won't find it as difficult to generate a passive income for yourself based on this option.

## How much can you potentially earn?

How much money you stand to make entirely depends on one thing - *you*. The more you sell, the more you make. It would also depend on the company that you're working with and the types of products you're selling. Established companies like Mary Kay and Avon for example, who already employ this distributed marketing approach, will most likely result in higher earning potential because the products have already established a reputation, compared to let's say a smaller, unknown brand or company perhaps. It could take a while before you start seeing a profit from the initial investment amount that you put in though, so you're going to need to be patient.

Anyone who is keen on making a little part-time money on the side can be involved in network marketing. What makes this option great is the combination of both the flexibility to choose your own hours, and you get a little bit of practice trying to run your own "business" in a way.

### Getting started with network marketing is easy, too:
- **Step 1 - Researching Your Company Options**: You need to decide which network marketing

company you would like to join and how to sign up. It is important that you spend some time researching the right company to work with, just like how you would invest the same amount of time deciding on which.

- **Step 2 - What's Your Why:** Network marketing is a business. Yes, it's working to generate passive income for you, but it's still a business nonetheless. Every entrepreneur who ventures into business must know their *why*, their reason for doing so, and so do you.

- **Step 3: Don't Skip the Trainings -** Once you've joined a network marketing company, take part in all the trainings and courses which are provided by the company, your mentor or your immediate supervisor. These opportunities offer great insight to help you get the most from your network marketing efforts.

- **Step 4: Advertise Yourself -** Once you've done all the above, the next step is to forget about being shy and just go for it. You must be confident enough in yourself and your products to be able to sell them. Introduce yourself, network, mingle, make connections, whatever opportunity comes your way, now is not the time to sit back and feel shy about it. Remember your *why* and your reason for doing this.

To answer the question, is network marketing a legitimate business? Yes, it is. It is *not a pyramid scheme,* which is a common myth associated with it because network marketing involves selling actual products. Unlike pyramid schemes that lure people in with the false promise of getting rich quickly with no basis for its claims, network marketing doesn't promise that you'll get rich through this approach, but it's good enough to bring in a little extra cash in your bank account.

# Idea #21 - Storage Rentals

## What is it?

Storage rentals are an excellent passive income option because of the "low maintenance and high returns" aspect. If you're looking for a piece of real estate to generate a steady source of passive income regularly, without forking out several hundred dollars or risking another mortgage payment buying a piece of property to rent, then storage rentals are easily your most affordable piece of real estate.

## Who is it for?

Two perks associated with passive income generation reflect the freedom and flexibility benefits that come along with it. With storage rentals, you have the best of both worlds, *and* you don't have to invest a lot of time and money upkeeping the facility the way you would with an apartment or a house. With the growing population, the demand for storage facilities is on the rise, especially in city locations where, sometimes, you simply don't have enough space to store all your belongings. Storage facilities, therefore, offer the perfect solution. You rent out your facility to tenants who come to store their stuff until such time where they no longer need this facility. If you've got a little bit of capital to spare to purchase a storage unit, and you're looking for a low-risk type of property investment that is easy to manage, the storage facility rentals are the answer that you seek.

Quite simply, storage rentals are where you have a storage facility located outside your home. What you do is that you then rent out this space to anyone who is looking for a facility to store their belongings. The level of security provided in these facilities would depend on the provider, but generally, they are safe. Units can be locked, and they're easily accessible 24-hours a day.

## How much could you potentially earn?

Storage facilities are one of the easiest ways for anyone to start creating a source of passive income. Financial experts like Robert Kiyosaki have even mentioned what a desirable investment option it is. How much money you stand to make would depend on several factors. Typically, storage facilities contain several hundred units in a single location, and these units can be rented out starting from $50 and upwards. The bigger your unit, the more you'll be able to charge.

**To get started renting out your storage unit, here's what you need to do:**

- **Step 1 - Purchase a Unit.** This is the most obvious way to get started. To rent out a unit, you must first *have* a unit.

- **Step 2 - Picking a Desirable Unit.** Your storage unit has to be appealing, or nobody is going to want to rent from you. When selecting a storage unit, some factors that you need to take into consideration include whether it's a climate-controlled unit, how accessible it is, the video monitoring facilities available, number of locks provided, whether in-person surveillance is available, size of the unit, overall safety and security, and lighting facilities. It's also a good idea to read online reviews about the facility before you make a commitment to it.

- **Step 3 - Advertise.** Start advertising your unit to get the word out that you've got a space to rent.

- **Step 4: Prepare a Contract.** A binding contract is needed to protect both your interests and that of the person who is renting your unit from you. A storage unit may not be an apartment or a house, but you are still essentially renting out a piece of property, and a rental agreement is still necessary.

- **Step 5: Checking If Permits Are Needed.** While most states generally do not require permits for any property that is less than 200 square feet, you should just do the same thing and check anyway if you'll need a permit for your storage facility.

- **Step 6: Get Insurance** - It's a good idea to get your storage unit covered by insurance just in case of any emergencies. It gives your renter peace of mind too, knowing that the facility you're providing is covered, if need be.

While providing storage rentals can be a great source of passive income, the myth that this type of passive income generator is a "cash cow" is exactly that - *a myth*. This choice is not an option you should go for if you're thinking about getting rich quick. This passive income source will generate some extra cash into your bank accounts.

It's also a myth that this is the "cheapest" business you can get into. While it's relatively low cost compared to a lot of other business models, depending on the location of your facility, it may not necessarily be as "cheap" as you think, especially when today's storage facilities are being constructed with higher quality material and provide a greater level of security. All these improvements are going to hike up the cost of your initial investment. So the term "cheap" really depends on the context. It's much more affordable if you're comparing it to purchasing a piece of property, but thinking that it's the "cheapest business to get into" is a myth that needs to be debunked.

## Idea #22 - Develop Design Elements

### What is it?

If you have a talent for design and you've got technology proficiency, developing design elements could be a great potential source of passive income for you. As a designer, you have the flexibility of options to increase your business without having to feel like you're piling up on your workload.

What's great about generating some passive income as a designer is that it reduces your dependency on clients to get paid. When you work as a freelance designer especially, it can be stressful constantly trying to search for clients, pitching your ideas, hoping they like your proposal and then going back and forth negotiating on the terms of payment.

Developing design elements that you can put up for sale on various platforms and online marketplaces, on the other hand, cuts out the bulk of your workload. You just need to design the content, put it up for sale, and anyone who's interested can purchase it immediately.

### Who is it for?

This passive income stream is ideal for anyone who's got a computer to work with, is creative with tons of ideas, design software, and some spare time to work on designing. it's the perfect option for anyone who's already working as a developer, or a designer and is looking to make a little extra income as a side hustle.

### How much money can you potentially earn?

How much money you potentially stand to earn from this would depend on the type of content you're selling and how often your content gets purchased. Another factor impacting your earning potential is the rates that you charge. More experienced, reputable designers have the luxury of charging slightly higher prices than those who have recently joined the scene. Design content can start anywhere from as low as $5 to $10 per content, and even be as much as a few hundred, depending on the quality and the intricacy of the work involved.

In the case of making passive income from developing design elements, the money you'll be earning is going to come repeatedly from the sale of one job. Recurring income is what makes it *passive* since you do no longer have to invest even more time working on developing and designing new content.

**How to do this?**

To start making passive income by developing design elements, here's what you can do:

- **Creating themes to sell on WordPress** - Designing themes and templates for platforms like WordPress is one way to go about producing a continuous income stream. The toughest part will be in the beginning, when you've got to come up with the ideas and put in the hours for the templates; but once you're done, each time someone purchases one of your templates, that's money in the bank for you.

- **Graphics To Be Used on Websites** - Another great option to consider, since there are new websites emerging all the time as new businesses and companies get formed. As long as websites exist, there will always be a need for graphics, and you could step in a fill that demand by developing these types of contents and creating a nice income stream for yourself while you're at it.

- **Selling Fonts** - Yes, there is even a demand for fonts. Develop and design fonts which are custom made, hand-drawn, in vector forms, airbrushed, fonts with extra characters, fonts which have embellishments, get creative and get designing.

- **Developing 3D Models -** 3D models are presently needed for all sorts of projects, so why not make a passive income option out of it? From animated models to architecture landscapes, if you've got a gift for designing and developing these elements, there could be a passive income opportunity in it for you.

- **Selling Stock Photography -** Design elements doesn't have to be focused on graphics or Photoshopping alone. Selling stock photography is another way of producing a "design" element to sell online. The only equipment you'll need is a good camera, a creative eye for what makes a good photo composition, take a fantastic picture and put it up for sale. That's recurring passive income for you whenever your images get purchased and used.

Passive income through developing design elements can be a great passive income stream, but as with any other passive income stream, this is something that is going to take time to build momentum. If anyone has told you that you could get rich quickly doing lots of design work, then that's a myth. The kind of income you generate will depend heavily on how often your content gets purchase. Sometimes, you may get a high volume of sales, and then there may be times when you might not make any sales at all for several weeks. If you're looking for a consistent passive income stream each month, you might have to consider diversifying your options instead of just focusing on developing design elements alone.

# Idea #23 - Website Domain Flipping

## What is it?

Considering domain flipping as a potential passive income avenue? Why not, when there's definitely potential in it? If you've never heard of website domain flipping before, the concept is simple. You basically purchase a domain name with the sole purpose of trying to sell it quickly at a much higher cost. It's similar to what some people do with real estate: they purchase home, fix it up and then sell it at a higher cost with the intention to make a little bit of profit. The key to being successful with domain flipping though is to be at the right place at the right time *and* to have a valuable domain in your possession if you're going to charge premium prices for it.

## Who is it for?

There are several reasons why anyone would want to buy domain names. Some purchase domains for the SEO value that they hold, others purchase them for events, current trends, and starting up new company websites. Some even purchase certain domain names because it happens to suit their business name much better. All of these little details are what you need to keep in mind when you start of making a go of this passive income idea. They'll help you tremendously when deciding which websites would make good purchases for future flipping.

## How does it work?

To start website domain flipping as a passive income, you'll need to first learn the ropes. If you were working in real estate, for example, you wouldn't just wake up one morning and start selling houses right away. You'll need to learn how the business works. In the website domain flipping world, you're going to be just like a real estate investor, except for websites instead of property. What you'll require for this passive income business is a keen eye for detail and what could potentially be profitable domain names and profitable websites.

The next step of the process is to set a budget. Setting a budget will help you narrow down the list of options available to you, so you can then choose one that best fits your needs. If you have the skills and the technical know-how, you can even build a website on your own, reducing the capital that you would need to initially invest. If you're on a really tight budget, this one is a great substitute for purchasing a domain or website which has already been established.

Once you've done that, you can then move onto the next part of the process, which is to decide what type of domain or website you intend to buy. Do you want to purchase something that is new? Or wait until you come across some expired domains you can quickly latch onto the resell? Expired domains can be found at ExpiredDomains.net. If you're building a website from scratch, you're going to need a reliable web host as a place to store your website files.

Deciding what type of website or domain you want to purchase is another tricky bit of the process. Ideally, you want to look for domains or websites which have the potential to be more lucrative, such as forums, Adsense monetized sites, review sites, niche, book, e-commerce, and membership sites. Once you've found a website to purchase, you then need to get it registered before you can start looking for a buyer.

**How much could you potentially earn?**

How much you could potentially earn with your domain website or domain flipping falls into two different categories. For domain names, the value in them is determined based on the SEO value, the age and how well your domain is going to meet the needs of the person who is buying it. Websites, on the other hand, have their value based on the current and potential revenue, traffic, SEO, content, and more.

If you're wondering where you could flip your domain or website, there are several marketplace options that you could choose from. Flippa, WarriorForum, and DigitalPoint are examples of where you could seek out a potential buyer. If your website is high performing enough, you should be able to flip it fairly quickly. Other than that, your avenues of selling include spreading the word through channels like social media, emailing your contacts, and advertising on marketplaces online.

## Myths about website domain flipping

The most common myths associated with this option are that people think you can be passive about flipping your website or domain. Unfortunately no, you can't. You still have to actively promote your website. You can't just sit back and hope the website is going to sell itself. Another common myth is that domain flipping is something that can be learned just like that (snaps fingers). Again, this isn't entirely true, because you're going to have to spend quite a bit of time learning the basics to master how this process works. It's time-consuming, but if you love it, it can be an enjoyable process, and the extra cash flow doesn't hurt either.

## Idea #24 - Selling T-Shirts Online

### What is it?

If there's one item that is universally accepted by men, women, and children everywhere, it's t-shirts. These items are a staple that *everyone* (no exaggeration here) owns at least one piece of, if not several. Take a look in your own cupboard and count how many t-shirts you own. Whether they're worn in the summer, underneath your jackets in the colder months, or for lounging about the house, t-shirts are a constant in everyone's wardrobe; in turn, selling t-shirts online is a great passive income idea. You're selling something that everyone needs, how could you go wrong?

### How much could you potentially earn from this?

Now, how much profit you stand to make per t-shirt is going to depend on what your initial cost is and which platform you're selling your t-shirts on. For example, if the cost of your t-shirt was about $12 on average, and you wanted to sell your t-shirts on Amazon. If you log into Amazon, you'll see that the suggested selling price for a t-shirt is $19.99. This means that you could potentially earn around $8 in profit from just one t-shirt alone. Depending on the volume of t-shirts you sell, the more you sell, the more you earn.

Is selling t-shirts online a good passive income idea? Yes, *but* this opportunity is not necessarily suitable for just anyone. The ones who are going to benefit most from selling t-shirts online as a passive income option are people who love being involved in sales, artists, illustrators, and designers because they've got the creative advantage of being able to design their own unique t-shirts without having to outsource that part of the business and anyone who is willing to commit the time and the effort to selling t-shirts online as an extra income stream.

## How does it work?

The beauty of selling t-shirts online though is the wide audience base that you have at your disposal. Men, women, teenagers, children, even babies, there are so many categories you could get involved in, potentially tripling your sale options. If you're looking to enter this business, here are the steps that you'll need to go through:

- **Step 1:** Find your niche market and who you intend to cater for? Are you only targeting a specific group? Or more than one? Where is your customer base located? What's the demographic that you're targeting?

- **Step 2:** Once you have identified your target audience, do your research to find a need that you can fulfill. What is it that is lacking right now? What does your audience want to see from you? What can you offer them that your competitor cannot?

- **Step 3:** Set-up your online store. With this, there are two ways that you can go about it. The first is to set up your own websites and the second is to sell on platforms like Amazon, eBay, Shopify, AliExpress, and more. It doesn't take long to set up and account either and if building a website from scratch is not your cup of tea, you could consider this option instead.

- **Step 4:** Be detailed in your product description and use as many keywords as possible. The more SEO-rich your content is, the better your chances of appearing in the first few pages of the search results that Google pings back to a customer who is searching for a product just like yours.

Among the challenges you might face with selling t-shirts online include having to constantly come up with fresh ideas that keep your target audience interested. Because t-shirts are purchased so often, and fashions come and go before you've even had a chance to blink sometimes, keeping your products fresh, on-trend, and in line with the current interest of your target market is how you keep them coming back for more. Another challenge is going to be, of course, the high competition. Google "online t-shirts for sale" or "buy online t-shirts" and you'll end up with more than a hundred thousand results listed in front of you. Competition is tough, and you're going to have to do a lot of hard work to get yourself in front of your customers, especially in the beginning when you're just starting to get traction and momentum.

**Myths concerning t-shirt selling**

Like with many passive income stream ideas, the biggest myth with selling t-shirts online is that it is a way for you to "get rich and get rich quick". It is not. It is going to take a while for you to build momentum, especially when you're not going to be the only person selling t-shirts online. There are literally *hundreds,* if not thousands, of other online shops and people who are selling t-shirts online, too. Bust out of that myth that it's going to be an easy side hustle business too, because it is not. Competition levels are high and if you want to make money, you're going to have to get active in promoting your merchandise for sale.

# Idea #25 - Placing Ads on Your Car

## What is it?

Population Reference Bureau revealed that on average, Americans tend to spend approximately 26 minutes daily commuting to work. If this is you and your means of transport involves a car, then you'll be happy to know that your car could potentially turn into a money-making vehicle. How? By letting companies *pay* you to advertise their ads on your car.

## Who is it for?

This business is perfect for anyone who owns a car, drives a lot, and doesn't mind being seen in a car with random advertisements which sometimes cover your entire vehicle. You've seen those cars driving around town before, and if you don't mind being one of them, placing ads on your car could prove to be a good little side income for you.

Carvertise is an example of a car company who pays drivers just like you for the privilege of being able to place their ads on your cars. The company works on developing ads with many local businesses and helps these businesses connect with drivers who are in the targeted area. You would first need to become approved as a Carvertise driver, and once that's done, the company will then began applying color wraps and decals on your car for an agreed time period. When you sign up with companies like Carvertise, you will be prompted to fill out information which reveals your location, the type of car you have, and what kind of daily mileage you cover. Carvertise has a minimum 25-mile per day minimum requirement, which must be met before you can sign up with them. Other companies may have slightly different requirements which must be fulfilled before you can begin earning money.

*Passive Income Ideas*

## How much could you potentially earn?

Now, here's how the money portion of this passive income option works - *the more you drive, the more you get paid.* That's because more driving increases your chances of exposure, which means businesses would be willing to pay more to those who cover more miles. Depending on the length of your commute, you could potentially earn anywhere from $100 to even $400 per month.

Another requirement from many of these companies warrants that your car still retains its factory paint job condition and that you have a clean driving record (you will be "representing" the business in a way, after all). Once you fulfill all the minimum requirements that the company is looking for, you can submit an application and the company will assess if you are a good fit for any of their upcoming campaigns. However, this process can sometimes take several weeks before you start getting anything going. Once you do get signed up with a campaign, however, the campaign can be anywhere from one month to six months.

When you sign up with these car companies to have ads placed on your car, often you don't actually get to choose the ad that you end up with. The company will decide this for you. However, if you feel like the ad is inappropriate for your car or it is not something you feel comfortable advertising, you can always choose to opt out. Once you and the company have come to an agreement about the ad which will be placed on your car, a scheduled time to meet with a specialist to wrap your car is the next step of the process. Don't worry about the decals or wraps damaging your car, because they are often made with adhesives specially designed not to damage or scratch your car's original paintwork. Once you're done with the campaign, simply make another appointment to have the wrap removed.

With this passive income option, you'll want to be careful of scammers, especially the ones who promise big cash returns in exchange for placing ads on your cars. If it sounds too good to be true, then it probably is. The warning signs to look out for these scammers are if they ask you to deposit your own money first or if the links provided have no contact information. Look for legitimate companies like Carvertise and avoid any company that requires any sort of "upfront payment" for you to get started.

# Idea #26- Using Instagram for Passive Income

**What is Instagram?**

Instagram, like many of today's social media platforms, offers businesses big and small the incredible opportunities to reach both massive audiences as well as the targeted audience to connect with them, engage them, and ultimately, convert them into customers. Instagram is a simplified version of Facebook albeit much more visual. It's all about posting photos and videos only.

However, the more and more brands join Instagram, the bigger the competition and the harder it is to stand out in a person's feed.

Instagram opened up its new ad feature in 2015, utilizing Facebook advertising's system. Accordingly, marketers and passive income entrepreneurs now have the ability to reach a niche segment of the population, which is currently at 800 million users and growing. Instagram ads have become an avenue for brands looking to increase their engagement and by extension, their profits, to the 500 million active users who use Instagram EVERY DAY.

**Who is it for?**

Are you passionate about a specific topic? Does your account acquire followers every single day and do you have plenty of traction on the content that you post from likes, shares, and follows? Are people commenting regularly on your post? Do you already own an online business? Or has a website or blog?

If you answered YES to one or more of the questions above, then you might want to think about using your Instagram platform as a source of income. In other words, you can become an Instagram influencer. You can use Instagram as a platform for affiliate marketing or use it to sell content such as hotel reviews, or sell your digital artwork or even quotes. The idea here is not to have thousands of followers but to sustain the most engaged followers. The more engaged they are, the better for your Instagram Marketing.

## How much money can you potentially earn?

While the figures you earn depends on the extent of the marketing you do on your Instagram profile, a survey conducted among 5,000 Instagram influencers showed that 42 percent of them were charged $200 to $400 per post. Brands want to engage or do business with people who have a following that is engaged, so they can know if your audience is engaged with you or the concentration of engagement you have by looking at your analytics.

## How does Instagram Marketing work?

- Define Your Target Audience: Who are you aiming to target through this platform? If you've already got a good idea of the kind of demographic you're going after, a good strategy to employ would be to start customer profiling. This will give you a better sense of what kind of content your target is after, the sort of hashtags they use and even what communities they are involved in on Instagram. Think of this stage as your due diligence. The more information and details you can gather to create your customer persona, the more definitive your advertising strategy will be.

- Define Your Objectives: The first question you should ask is what does your business hope to achieve by advertising on Instagram? What can you do on Instagram that you cannot with other social media platforms? How does this platform integrate with your other social media platforms and marketing strategy?

Ideally, your objectives should try to increase brand awareness among your target audience, showcase your brand and company culture, shine the spotlight on your products and services (and why they're different), increase audience engagement and inspire brand loyalty. Your objectives should also seek to build a community that is more engaged, connect your brand with both audiences and influencers, increase sales by driving traffic to your site, and more. Your objectives will be the ones to help you navigate and decide on the next course of action.

- Use Your Hashtags Strategically. Before every post is sent out, ask yourself how many hashtags do you think would be best? Plus, which of these hashtags is going to benefit your ad the most? Having a quick think about these questions will save you a lot of time and prevent you from blindly hashtagging every word which you may think is going to help your post. Go with popular hashtags, but not the ones which are too popular where you run the risk of being lost in the tsunami of other content. 65,000 Instagram posts were analyzed by TrackMaven. This study discovered that if you want your post to receive the highest possible engagement rate, then 9 hashtags was the way to go.

- Building Brand Awareness (Goal): To achieve this goal, the accompanying advertising increases your reach and engagement by boosting your posts. For example, you could create a business ad that is aimed at the people closest to your business vicinity and try to reach as many people as possible. Creating ads which help your audience understand the value of your brand is a good way to start increasing brand awareness, especially among new customers.

## Myths about Instagram Marketing

1 - Do not use hashtags

Instagram uses hashtags to curate content specific to its audience. Users also use hashtags to find content. It works both ways. Many people say that hashtags make content messy but in this day and age, people aren't worried about hashtags simply because they've become an everyday part of life. Also, hashtags help people find, so unless you are Kim Kardashian, use the appropriate and targeted hashtags for your content.

2 - Follow everyone, so they will follow you back.

This is not entirely true. It helps that you follow people on Instagram, but this has to be the kind of people that you find their content interesting, people that you can learn from, the people who also surf the same wave you are on so you can see what they are doing. You can also follow people outside your area of interest. Whatever it is, follow them with a purpose and not randomly follow, connect, and engage with them for the sole purpose of increasing your follower account.

3 - If you have plenty of followers, you don't need to use Instagram Ads.

Instagram has a huge audience growth and every day, someone is opening a new account or connecting their business page to their Instagram. A survey conducted by Instagram assessed over 400 campaigns worldwide on ad recall, Instagram's ad recall was 2.8 times higher than that of other online advertising channels. Just because you have a high follower count does not mean that they're all entirely engaged with your content and posts. Using ads is a great

*Passive Income Ideas*

way to ensure you not only engage with your existing users but it also enables you to reach out to newer target audiences. Also, unless you are Kim Kardashian, use Instagram ads.

# Idea #27- Facebook Marketing

## What is it?

It's 2018 and by now, you know that everywhere you look on the internet; you will be bombarded with ads. One of the biggest ways the Internet knows what you like, what your last search was on your browser, who you are friends with, what articles you clicked on, and what was your last online purchase was through Facebook. One of the biggest ads popping up everywhere you look is Facebook ads. So what are they? We see them all the time, but do we know anything about them?

## Who is it for?

If you're planning to reach a wider audience, you might want to rethink and focus your marketing efforts to include Facebook as well. Facebook is another great way to spread your ideas, create ads to increase leads and sales, and also, include it into your affiliate marketing. If you're a person who loves social media platforms, you prefer marketing online and most of your audience uses Facebook, then this platform is feasible for passive marketing.

## How much money can you potentially earn?

Essentially, you make money through the ads that you create on Facebook. Facebook ads can be categorized according to i) Ads and ii) Sponsored stories. For example, you sell a product for $100 through your website. Each sale you make gives you a clear profit of $100. So long as you spend less than $100 on Facebook advertising your product, you make a positive ROI. Through Facebook Ads, you can increase your sales reach to a massive crowd if you target your ads to the right people, the right market, and with the right location.

## How does Facebook marketing work?

*Passive Income Ideas*

To start advertising on Facebook, you'll be required to have a Business Manager account that enables you to manage at least one Facebook Page.

### Step 1 - Setting Up Your Ad Account Info

Facebook will not allow you to start spending unless there is a value payment connected and some relevant business information shared. To set up your account, click on 'Ad Account Settings' on your Business Manager.

### Step 2 - Identifying your Facebook Audiences

You need to use this convenient Facebook tool called 'Audience Manager Tool' to create niche audiences and manage these different categories. This tool is found in the Business Manager application at the Audiences Tab.

### Step 3 - Location and Demographics Targeting

Facebook also allows you to target people in specific locations as well as through demographics. When you click on the Demographics tab, you find even more targeting topics to refine your audience based on age, gender, and location. Refine your audience using these filters.

### Step 4- Creating your ads

Here are the different types of ads that you can create with Facebook ads. There are a total of 10 different types that fall into the ad category:

- Mobile App ad
- Page post photo ad
- App ad
- Domain ad

- Page Like ad
- Page Post video ad
- Event ad
- Page Post Ads
- Page Post Link ad
- Page Post Text ad
- Offer ad

**Step 4 - Reviewing your campaign performance**

The Facebook Ad Manager is the easiest way to review your campaign performance. By using the ad manager, you can filter your campaigns by the dates, its objectives, and also zooming in on any campaign to see its performance based on its ad set.

**Myths about Facebook Marketing**

- **Facebook's algorithms will always be the same** - The rules of social media are rapidly changing so making the assumption that you cannot embrace it is your own downfall. If you want to continue passively earning an income through actively using Facebook to push sales, then you must always keep abreast of its every changing algorithm, your ever-changing audience, the evolving industry, and how your business is adapting to it.
- **Facebook marketing is always going to be free** - Since Facebook is now public, the only way it can monetize from its platform is through ads. Facebook will continue looking for ways to create its continuous river of gold, which means if you want to continue your revenue stream, you need to start reaching into your pocket even more.

*Passive Income Ideas*

# Idea #28- Create a Podcast

### What it is?

Podcasts are commonly known as on-demand internet radio. You can listen to a podcast on any digital device so long as it's connected to the internet. The word "podcast" is a combination of the word 'pod' and 'broadcast.'

### How much money can you potentially earn?

On an average basis, you can earn a minimum of $25 a month and up to even $820 a month based on what you're podcasting as well as the through programs that offer podcasting such as through Amazon Affiliate, Patreon as well as through Sponsors.

### How it works - Step-by-Step

While the steps to do a podcast are a little bit more elaborate, here is the high-level outlook to how you can start a podcast:

1. Choose a topic you can commit to.
2. Define your show description and artwork.
3. Set up and thoroughly test your equipment.
4. Create a plan for your episodes.
5. Record your episodes.
6. Edit and publish your episodes.
7. Launch your podcast to your audience.

### Myths about Podcasting

- Podcasting is a niche medium - many mainstream media keep spreading the fact that podcasting is niche and has a small audience. While there is some truth in

*Passive Income Ideas*

it, that podcasts have a niche audience, with the internet, more and more people are turning to on-demand networks for their source of entertainment and information. Take Netflix, for example. If Netflix is extremely popular for TV content, then podcasts are the radio version.

- If your content is good, you'll attract listeners - Your listeners need more than just good content. For your podcasts to work, you need to ensure that content, style, and production all work in tandem so you can produce quality audio material. Content is key but delivering it in a quality way is also essential.

- Finding podcasts is hard - You've probably seen tabs on your favorite streaming channels that have 'Podcasts' shown. The truth is, it's now much easier to find and listen to podcasts than ever before especially with the majority of content available via mobile devices. Services such as Netflix, Spotify as well as iTunes, all have features where you can listen to podcasts.

# Idea #29 - Buy an Existing Online Business

## What it is?

Online business or e-commerce is a platform for buying and selling services and products over the Internet. An online business can encompass the following business models:

- Online shopping
- Business-to-business buying and selling
- Online financial exchanges for trading and forex
- Business-to-business (B2B) electronic data interchange

If you're interested in building a passive income via online businesses, it's best that you start with buying over existing sites than to start one on your own. Many successful individuals that are into online businesses generate a huge part of the revenue stream from purchasing and owning multiple businesses at one time. Not to discourage you from starting your own website, but like any business, it'll take time before it starts to generate cash and become profitable. As such, the next alternative is to buy an existing business that is for sale.

## Who is it for?

It needs to be pointed out that buying an existing online business doesn't guarantee that you will make money right of the get-go. Just like an investment, it does take some effort and time to maintain and grow the business before you start seeing profits. As such, if you possess these criteria, then you should definitely consider dwelling into this type of passive income stream:

- Someone who is interested in developing and growing the business.
- Someone who has experience operating and growing online businesses and knows what it takes to keep them sustainable.
- Someone with a high-risk tolerance looking for a challenging project.
- Someone who has the money and energy to invest in buying and operating an existing online business.
- Someone who knows how to evaluate an existing business' strengths and weaknesses

## How much money can you potentially earn?

In 2017, online businesses were reportedly just made up about 9% of the total retail sales in the U.S, but it is projected to reach about $414 billion by the end of 2018. In general, the best way to generate income from online business platforms is by the use of advertisements. Some businesses have been known to grow and generate revenue from $1,000 per month to $2,000 per months. Some have even gone up to $5,000 per month, but this will generally depend on the size of the community and traffic going into the said website.

## How it works - Step-by-Step

If you're keen on purchasing an existing online business to diversify your income stream, you'll need to establish some key parameters on what you need to look out for and what would fit you and your goals. Here are some points that you should be exploring:

Product: Determine the type of product or service that you would be interested in and source for businesses that sell these kinds of items.

Market Niche: Going for a product that is a niche or serves a particular segment would definitely be a benefit to your business.

Be Industry Specific: Try to leverage your experience for a given market or industry. It could be something you have previously worked on or even a hobby you are passionate about.

Business Size: Try to source for a business that already has an existing customer base, employees, and distribution locations.

Profit and Income Generated: You may also want to seek businesses that are already generating healthy profits that are in line with your objectives and goals.

Healthy Customer Base: Always locate businesses that have a large and more importantly growing customer base.

**Myths about online business**

Before you dive into buying an online business, it's best to take a look at the most common myths or misconceptions associated with it:

- Work part-time to make a full-time income - Like any new business; the start usually will require a large amount of time and hard work to get it going and to generate revenue. It takes time to grow a business and create a sustainable income.

- It's easy with social media - The social media platforms have provided online businesses with an opportunity to reach out to a wider audience. But with any marketing strategy, it is important that any marketing campaign done to promote your business needs to target your intended market and demographics.

- Starting an online business is free - Unfortunately, this is only half-truth. While starting an online business or buying on is relatively easier than your traditional business, it still requires some capital investment to buy the business and maintain it.

# Idea #30- Franchise a Business

## What it is?

A franchise is, in simple terms, a licensing relationship. A company like Baskins or Starbucks usually operates this way by licensing its brand and operating systems to interested individuals. As such, the company gives you the rights to sell their products; in turn, you agree to pay certain a percentage of fees upfront and follow their conditions and guidelines. Examples of franchises are:

- Petrol kiosks
- Fast food restaurants
- Coffee houses

## Who is it for?

A franchise business based on a passive income stream can suit most people, but it depends primarily on the individual on how long and often one wants to invest the time and effort into it. As such, one can balance his or her lifestyle and commitments to suit the needs of the franchise system. For example, one passive income franchise known as Xpresso Delight has over 150 franchisees and the operators are anywhere between 20 to 60 years of age.

## How much money can you potentially earn?

The question of how much money can be potentially earned from a franchise business will roughly depend on the particular franchise's industry. As such, here is a list of various franchises to denote their required investment and their respective net-worth:

**7-Eleven**

*Passive Income Ideas*

Description: Convenience store

Type of Business: Brick and mortar
Minimum Investment Required: $34,550
Net-worth Requirement: $100,000
Franchise Fee: $10,000
Royalty Fee: none, profit sharing

**Planet Fitness**

Description: Gym and fitness facility focusing on occasional or first-time gym users
Type of Business: Brick and mortar
Minimum Investment Required: $728,000
Net-worth Requirement: $3,000,000
Franchise Fee: $10,000
Royalty Fee: 5%

**Two Men and a Truck**

Description: Local packing and moving company
Type of Business: In-home service
Minimum Investment Required: $178,000
Net-worth Requirement: $350,000
Franchise Fee: $50,000
Royalty Fee: 6%

**The Learning Experience**

Description: Education-based childcare services
Type of Business: Brick and mortar
Minimum Investment Required: $495,299
Net-worth Requirement: $500,000
Franchise Fee: $60,000
Royalty Fee: 7%

**How it works - Step-by-Step**

Anyone looking to generate passive income via a franchise is definitely seeking a work-life balance as the main criteria. As such, there are two major prerequisites when deciding on what type of franchise you should enter.

You'll first need to identify a business that allows you to work from home, or in other words, use your home as an office space. This will allow you to spend more time with your family and doing the things you like instead of commuting from one place to another. Next, you would want to look out for a business that allows flexibility in terms of the hours that you put into it. This will enable you to balance time between other commitments and allow for greater efficiency into the schedule.

**Myths**

There are a number of misconceptions regarding owning a franchise. As such, here are some of the myths usually associated with it:

- You'll only be successful with the right business – Never limit yourself to what you're only good at. Explore various opportunities that require the same skill set or learn new ones to make your business successful.

- I need to quit my day job – Many current franchise systems provide flexibility in the work time arrangements. Also, many franchise owners are more passive than full-time investors.

- I'm unable to afford a franchise – Some franchises can be bought for anything less than $100,000 and some can go for as little as $10,000. You just need to conduct in-depth research and planning to find one that fits your commitments.

## Idea #31- Rent out your clothes

### What is it?

Apart from evening gowns and tuxedos, many people are now looking to even rent everyday wear instead of splashing money on clothes that they would otherwise wear only once in their lifetime. As such, if you have items in your closet just hanging around, you might want to consider renting them out instead of putting them in the trash. What used to be a taboo is currently becoming a trend, especially among women. Here are a few websites that allow you to rent out your clothes:

- <u>DateMyWardrobe</u>: You can rent out clothing, shoes, and accessories.
- <u>StyleLend</u>: They have <u>specific brands</u> they accept.
- <u>RentezVous</u>: Currently in beta, mostly available in London and Paris.

### Who is it for?

Basically, if you have any pieces of clothing that you are not going to use or even those that have been in your closet for a number of years, you can start to rent them out. And it can also be extended to other accessories such as purses, heels, and any other types of attires.

### How much money can you potentially earn?

There isn't much available data on the market about the profitability of clothes sharing platforms. But one popular site indicated how those who rent out their clothes and accessories cap the rental between 5-10% of the retail price for that item. So, your income stream will depend on two factors which are:

- How many items you have listed
- How often those items get rented

So, getting more items into your list will be a plus point to increase the rental likelihood. Also, having a wide array of outfits to fit many different sizes will also help.

## How It Works - Step-by-Step

Stylelend.com is one website that provides a platform for online clothing rental to the general public. Once you're registered with them and it's approved, you can begin to list your items on there. Should anyone be interested in renting your piece of clothing, you will be notified of it, and then you'll need to prepare it for shipping. For Stylelend.com, it's vital to know that you can only list items of clothing under designer brands and not clothing from companies like Zara, H&M, and TopShop.

## Myths

There are a number of misconceptions regarding clothing rental. As such, here are some of the myths usually associated with it:

- Options are usually out of season – Most platforms constantly update their collection to ensure it's within the season and not out of style.
- Dry-Cleaning – Most platforms ensure that the garments are dry-cleaned before they reach you, so you only need to ensure that there's no damage to the condition of the clothing upon return.

# Idea #32- Develop WordPress Themes

## What is it?

For WordPress, a theme is a group of templates that are used to enhance an appearance and general outlook of a WordPress website. It can be changed to suit the intended style of the user, whenever needed. WordPress.org has a huge database of these themes in their directory. Each theme has a specific layout, feature, and design. You can then select one that fits your website from these directories. Since there's a market for various types of WordPress themes, many developers have found a way to generate income by selling WordPress themes.

## Who is it for?

You may think that since WordPress is a web-based platform that only expert web developers can create and market their unique themes; however, it may come as a surprise that creating WordPress themes aren't limited to those with web design knowledge. Creating a WordPress theme that suits your specific requirements is relatively straightforward. And it doesn't require a lot of technical knowledge or experience with web development.

## How much money can you potentially earn?

ThemeForest is a platform designed for selling WordPress themes, and in 2008, they recorded around $280,000 worth of transactions just on WordPress themes alone. According to Vivek Nanda, a creator of PaySketch, developers are making around $200-300K per year on selling WordPress themes. But he also warned there are many who don't even make any income from the themes they have designed.

## How it works - Step-by-Step

The amount of revenue you generate from your WordPress theme will depend based on the category of your theme, your competitors, and how effectively you market your themes. Therefore, here are some key essentials when starting on this venture:

- Have a good product – Always work towards having a theme that offers a feature that no one else or performs better than your competitor. Being unique and able to meet the requirements of the intended recipient is a sure-fire way to get ahead of the game.

- Affordable Pricing – Having a theme that's too expensive will drive away would-be buyers, as such; it is advisable that you begin by pricing your themes around $20-$30 as a start. This will, in turn, attract more customers to your themes.

- Marketing Plan – You need to spend a good amount of time to ensure that your product reaches its intended customer base. Get a blog running, advertise your product on your social media account, and also, it will be advantageous if you can start a website to promote your themes.

- Ensure continuous support and updates – Always ensure that you provide your customers with constant tech support and updates. This will provide repeat sales and make you stand out from your competition.

## Myths

There are a number of misconceptions regarding WordPress. As such, here are some of the myths usually associated with it:

- WordPress isn't a blogging tool. It's a website builder that is used by more than 31% of websites on the Internet.
- WordPress is not secure. In contrary, it is very secure; hence, its popularity among developers.
- It doesn't support E-Commerce. WordPress has many plug-ins that provide E-Commerce functionality.

## Idea #33- Launch a Webinar

### What it is?

A webinar is online seminars that are crafted to teach or disseminate information around a specific topic. Most webinars are around 30 to 40 minutes and are viewed by those wanting to learn, see a demo about a product, see new feature or updates, gather tips and hacks as well as best practices. Webinars are also a perfect way to introduce yourself to your audience.

### Who is it for?

Webinars are great for people who have something to share. Are you a lecturer and you want to share your content or your teaching materials to students not in your location? Are you a teacher with plenty of online content and you'd like to help students learn without coming to you physically?

Are you a mental coach or a business coach with a target audience wanting to hear your secrets of success? Or are you an industry expert who has plenty of business ideas to share? All of these make you a perfect candidate to launch a webinar. Basically, as long as you have information and content to share, you can use a webinar to launch yourself to your audience.

### How much money can you potentially earn?

You can make money by getting people to pay before attending your webinar or if it's a free webinar, which is what most people offer, you have to offer a paid product or service at the end. Your audience can then purchase your product or service and also take back the lessons they have learned.

If you promote your webinar properly, disseminated your information to your audience in a proficient way, and your attendees have learned well from you, then they'll definitely purchase your product on the spot.

*Passive Income Ideas*

At the very least, you should be charging your audience $100 per person because it takes about $100 to produce a webinar and pay for other costs of set up.

**How to launch a webinar?**

There are several paid and free hosting sites available for you to consider and depending on what site you choose, there will be some form of technical assistance or step-by-step guide to help you create and launch your webinar. Below is a more synthesized version that can give you an idea of what it takes to launch a webinar:

1. Settle on a specific topic
2. Pick the right webinar format for your content
3. Plan your SEO and promotion strategies to inform your audience
4. Consider time zones
5. Create clear, persuasive, and directional slides
6. Test your signal, audio, and video equipment
7. Run a test webinar days ahead and few hours ahead
8. Write a strong script
9. Prep your recording area suitable with the topic
10. Don't forget to hit record!
11. Have an official hashtag

**Myths about Launching a Webinar**

- I just need to build a webinar and people will come!

    Attracting the relevant audience is by far the biggest challenge of your webinar. People will come to your webinar if your topic is genuine and it aims to educate and inform prospects or solve an issue or even help them to achieve better results in a specific topic. If your content is a 'nice to have,' chances are your prospective audience will ignore your email or even unsubscribe from it.

- I'm great at doing presentations, I'll just wing it!

  The virtual world is vastly different from that of the real, in-person one. And one of the major issues faced in webinars is connectivity issues with regards to internet connectivity, audio, and visual connectivity as well. When people find it hard to hear you, they'll tend to leave. If there are awkward silences or dead air, people will leave. You must use the tech tools efficiently and your slides need to be more directional than the ones you use in live presentations.

- Your audience is ready to buy

  Plenty of buyers do their research first before even attending a webinar. This is an unrealistic expectation and when it does not happen, there's a severe disappointment. Many of the people who register for your webinar are in various stages of buying, and most of them are looking for more information and just want to be educated. They're less likely to purchase a product from you by the end of your webinar. So, your main goal here is to ensure that the right information is given to your audience who came to find out more, not to buy more.

## Idea #34- Give Fashion & Product Reviews

### What it is?

With online platforms available to anyone who wants to create a profile, it's given people a new channel to voice out their opinions, give feedback, and seek answers. People are quick to channel their happiness as well as grievances with a brand on social media. Love a recent hotel you stayed in? Let's review them on TripAdvisor. Don't like the service at the Italian restaurant down your street? Let's review them on Yelp. Checking to see if a certain brand of vacuum cleaner works as advertised? Check Amazon reviews.

Reviews are a major source of information for plenty of people to judge whether a product or service does what it says or delivers its brands' promises which is why blogs and websites such as AliExpress, Amazon, and Ulta have a review section on their sites.

But what if you want more personal answers? Well, some people have turned to review fashion and beauty product on their own social media platforms and managed to amass a huge following of fans who want to hear and see what they have to say. Giving fashion and beauty product reviews are a lucrative passive income stream because there's a guaranteed following already.

### Who is it for?

It's for anyone who is purveyors of fashion and beauty products who knows what works and what doesn't. If you love anything fashion and beauty and you see yourself purchasing a fair bit of products, you can definitely start giving your reviews as well. Users of today prefer hearing first-hand reviews of products to signify better credibility and greater transparency of a product or service.

## How much money can you potentially earn?

On an average basis, you can sign up as testers and reviewers at places such as FameBit or CrowdTap or even Modern Mom where you can see yourself earning about $50 to $75 for the reviews you make. Some people have even gone to their own social media channels to make videos to inform their audience what they think of a product. As their audience grows, brands take notice and request for their own products to be reviewed. The reviewer can then charge them a certain sum for the number of views the video receives.

## How it works - Step-by-Step

So, how do you get started on writing reviews? If you're not a fan of increasing your audience on social media, you can start creating your foundations as a reviewer on sites that pay you for writing reviews.

- Firstly, you can check out sites such as SwagBucks, Inbox Dollars, or Vindale Research.
- Next, you need to open an account with them. Follow the steps to sign up and provide the necessary verification information. Each site will have different verification as well as a rewards system. Swagbucks, for instance, provides its members with free gift cards and cash for daily things that they already do online.
- Depending on the reward criteria, you need to shop online or watch videos, or search the web, or answer surveys to redeem your points.
- When you've collected enough points, you can redeem these points as gift cards with online merchants such as Walmart or Amazon. You can also opt to get Cashback from PayPal.

# Idea #35- Help Someone Learn a Language through Skype

## What it is?

Skype is the latest communication tool that provides the ability to make video chats and voice calls between computers, tablets, and mobile devices over the Internet. Due to this technological advancement, there has been a huge growth in teaching language over the Internet. Plus, this opens up a limitless border as you can engage individuals from different continents and increase your revenue stream. Apart from that, Skype is also cheaper, more accessible, and it can be done from the comfort of your home.

## Who is it for?

Well, if you're already proficient in a language or two, you're good to go. All you need now is a laptop and an Internet connection.

## How much money can you potentially earn?

LiveLingua.com, a language tutoring website that uses Skype, charges $20 - $25 per hour based on the type of language course taken. Hence, the logic here will be to get as many students as you possibly can to generate higher revenue of income.

## How does it work?

Here is a look at the various steps that you need to take in order to dwell into the teaching language online:

- Decide if you're going to teach in your mother tongue or another foreign language where you also possess proficiency.
- Know your purpose. Is it to make more money or connect with other language learners or to challenge yourself in new ventures? This will ensure that you are always motivated.
- You may want to begin your online tutoring journey by offering free classes as a start to build your base and confidence.
- Ensure that you use all avenues at your disposal to market yourself and your services. Use social media, blog, or websites to promote your language classes.
- Once you start getting more students, it's important that you build a lesson plan or syllabuses for your students. Have practice lessons that your students can work on in their free time.

**Myths about Teaching through Skype**

There are a number of misconceptions regarding online language tutoring. As such, here are some of the typical myths usually associated with it:

- Learning a language is difficult – Learning and teaching a new language isn't difficult. It just takes time.
- You have to live in the country that language is spoken – If you have a laptop and Internet connection, you can learn any language from the comfort of your home.
- Only children can learn a new language – Not true. Adults can also pick up a new language as long as the desire is there.
- Language can only be taught in a classroom environment – Once again, if this was true, then many courses that

prestigious universities offer online will have to be closed down. As long as the course content is structured and organized, with well-planned tutorials and exercises, anyone can teach a language.

# Conclusion

Based on the new economy, merged with the Internet, we have numerous ways to earn an income. Passive income is a great way to earn extra money to pay our bills, make ends meet, and even fund our travels with little input on our end. You also don't need to quit your day job to do so because most passive income stream explained in this book is ideal to be conducted on an online basis.

What's even better is that you can use whatever skills you already pose to kick-start a passive income stream or use the many different platforms that enable you to make money such as through self-publishing, affiliate marketing, and even Cashback rewards.

Although the premise of passive income is to contribute as little effort as possible to bring in your income, you still need to exert your time and a considerable amount of work to build up the foundations, so that you can reap your passive income later.

The business ideas listed in this book enable you to start generating passive income fairly quickly, but take note that none are get-rich-quick schemes.

With time, effort, and maybe a little bit of monetary investment, your passive income business will earn you a pretty good amount of money over time.

# Thank you

Before you go, I just wanted to say thank you for purchasing my book.

You could have picked from dozens of other books on the same topic but you took a chance and chose this one.

So, a HUGE thanks to you for getting this book and for reading all the way to the end.

Now I wanted to ask you for a small favor. **Could you please consider posting a review on the platform? Reviews are one of the easiest ways to support the work of independent authors.**

This feedback will help me continue to write the type of books that will help you get the results you want. So if you enjoyed it, please let me know!

Lastly, don't forget to grab a copy of your Free Bonuses *"The Fastest Way to Make Money with Affiliate Marketing" and "Top 10 Affiliate Offers to Promote".* Just go to the link below.

https://theartofmastery.com/chandler-free-gift

Printed in Poland
by Amazon Fulfillment
Poland Sp. z o.o., Wrocław